A Chronological Outline
of
World Theatre

A Chronological Outline
of
World Theatre

by
Walter J. Meserve
and
Mollie Ann Meserve

FEEDBACK THEATREBOOKS FTPP & PROSPERO PRESS

Manufactured in the United States of America.

Feedback Theatrebooks & Prospero Press
305 Madison Avenue Suite 1146
New York, NY 10165

ISBN 0-937657-12-3

Table of Contents

Origins of Theatre

Where, when and how did theatre originate, and what constitutes a drama? These questions are not easily answered and never to the complete satisfaction of all people. Scholars agree that in addition to shamanistic rituals, storytelling and puppets are seminal influences upon the development of theatre in the Orient. No one knows exactly where puppetry originated -- India? China? -- and storytelling seems to have no definable beginning. There are, however, three suggestions for the origins of theatre that most scholars acknowledge. There are the traditional shamans, male and female, who claim or are endowed with supernatural powers and maintain their status through native wit and performance abilities. There are celebrations and festivals in which people participate for religious or secular reasons. And there are those characteristics of self-indulgent human nature which compel people to entertain themselves and others by imitating their world, human or animal, or by revealing and boasting of personal skills or possessions through singular performances. All theatre depends in one way or another upon these human resources.

W.J.M
M.A.M.

Theatre of the Ancient Oriental World,
3000 B.C.-801 B.C.

EGYPT   INDIA

3000 B.C.
   3100-2686 B.C. Early Dynastic Period
   Hieroglyphic Writing
   The Great Pyramids
   "Pyramid Texts" Rituals   2700-1500 B.C. Indus Valley
   Coronation Plays   Civilization
   Ramesseum Dramatic Papyrus
2500 B.C.
   2686-2181 B.C. Old Kingdom
   The Triumph of Horus
   Memphite Drama
   Abydos Passion Play
2000 B.C.   2133-1786 B.C. Middle Kingdom
   Classical Literature
   New musical instruments
   Entertainments

1500 B.C.   1500-1200 B.C. Aryans invade
   1517-1085 B.C. New Kingdom   Indian Sub-Continent
   Thriving Literature, *Books of the Dead*   *Rig Veda*
   1350 B.C. Beginning of Decline of
      Egyptian Civilization

1000 B.C.
   1085-341 B.C. Late Dynastic Period
   Beginning of Cultural Renaissance   850-650 B.C. Great War
   Persia conquers Egypt   (later depicted in
   Greeks expel Persians   *Mahabharata)*

Theatre of the Ancient Oriental World,
3000 B.C.-801 B.C.

CHINA

KOREA

3000 B.C.

2500 B.C.

2333 B.C. Dan-Gun (1st
legendary king)
Dance and music begin

2205-1767 B.C. Hsia Dynasty
(legendary)

2000 B.C.

1767-1122 B.C. Shang Dynasty

1500 B.C.

c.1333 B.C-494 A.D. Kingdom
of Buyo
Festival of *Yong-Go*,
Welcoming of the Drum

c. 1122-255 B.C. Chou Dynasty
Shamanistic Rituals from
dynastic records
Book of Odes

1000 B.C.

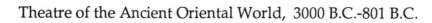

Theatre of the Ancient Oriental World, 3000 B.C.-801 B.C.

EGYPT

• Ancient texts of the Early Dynastic Period (3100-2686 B.C.) indicate a theatrical activity involving enactment, dialogue and enough dramatic conventions to distinguish the Egyptian culture as having the oldest drama in the world.

• "Pyramid Texts" (Early Dynastic Period) dealt with a king's death and may have been enacted during the king's lifetime. In one "Pyramid Text" a king claims his right as Horus: "O Geb, bull of the sky, I am Horus, my father's heir."

• *The Ramesseum Dramatic Papyrus* (Early Dynastic Period), discovered in 1895-86, is both a ritual or *Heb Sed* play of the legend of Osiris, celebrating a king's jubilee, and a Coronation Play, celebrating the elevation of a king to the throne, performed in 46 scenes at designated stations during a royal cruise down the Nile River.

• *The Triumph of Horus* (Old Kingdom, 2686-2181 B.C.) is the best example of the Egyptian ritual drama. Every king of Egypt became Horus, the son of Osiris and Isis. This play formed part of the annual Festival of Victory, commemorating the war between Seth, the evil spirit, and Horus and the victory of Horus and his coronation as king of United Egypt. A scene in this play showing the hippopotamus might have involved references to the god Baes (god of procreation) and his consort, the hippopotamus goddess of pregnancy, who would provide comic relief in later serious plays.

• *The Memphite Drama* (Old Kingdom), a fragment, inscribed on the "Shabako Stone," was evidently part of an annual festival taking place on the first day of spring. It tells how Geb, god of the earth, tried to end the conflict between Horus and Seth by giving Lower Egypt to Horus and Upper Egypt to Seth before reversing his decision and giving all to Horus.

• *The Abydos Passion Play* (Old Kingdom) is concerned with the mysteries of creation, life, death and the conflict between good and evil. It dramatized the death and dismemberment of Osiris by his brother Seth, the scattering of his body parts throughout the land, the birth of his son, Horus, and Osiris' resurrection to eternal life when his body is reassembled by Isis and Horus. The ritual was performed from 2500 B.C. to 500 B.C.

• New musical instruments were introduced during the period of the Middle Kingdom (2133-1786 B.C.). Egyptians enjoyed frequent holidays involving ceremonies, parades and amusements. Their extreme fondness of music was evident at all celebrations, which might include acrobats, jugglers, magicians and storytellers. One of the earliest folk tales, "The Shipwrecked Sailor," comes from the 12th Dynasty.

• *Books of the Dead* (New Kingdom) were papyrus rolls on which certain magic spells were written. They were buried with Egyptians who expected to have the spells recited for them in the next world.

INDIA

• The Indus Valley Civilization (2700-1500 B.C.) is one of the earliest sophisticated and artistic societies of the world. Siva, the god of actors and dancers, was a central figure for these people. Seemingly, as part of religious rituals, they enjoyed music and dancing.

• The *vedas* (1500-500 B.C.) reflect the principal religious ideas introduced by the Aryans who destroyed the Indus Valley Civilization. After centuries of oral transmission, the hymns, rituals and philosophical treatises were written down in Veddic, the parent language of Sanskrit.

• Rituals existed and perhaps also entertainments, but there is no evidence of a developing theatre. Some of the hymns in the *vedas*, however, are written in brief dialogue which could have been interpolated in a liturgical manner.

CHINA

• Shamans and Shamanesses enacted rituals and performed as singers, dancers and impersonators during the Chou Dynasty (1122-255 B.C.). Ceremonial dances and gesture, inseparable from dance in Asia, are basic to theatre in China, where the actor is more important than the play.

• Certain poems from the *Book of Odes* (Chou Dynasty, 1122-255 B.C.), chanted and accompanied by music, suggest action that is comparable to the liturgical drama of Europe during the middle ages.

KOREA

• According to legend, Dan-Gun (2333 B.C.), mythical founder who established the first civilization on the peninsula, worshipped Hanunin, Lord of Heaven, and celebrated the gods of the earth with dancing and music.

• *Yong-Go* (Kingdom of Buyo, c.1333 B.C-494 A.D.), a religious festival for the worship of the Lord of Heaven, was celebrated by the people in the 10th month of each year with singing, dancing and wine drinking -- comparable to the Greek celebration of Dionysus.

Theatre of the Pre-Christian World, 800 B.C.-301 B.C.

EGYPT	INDIA
800 B.C.	Later *vedas* Early *upanishads*
700 B.C.	
600 B.C.	
	Gautama Buddha (c. 563-488 B.C.)
525-405 B.C. Persian conquest of Egypt	
500 B.C.	
c. 450 B.C. Herodotus visits Egypt	
400 B.C.	Kautilya, *Artha Sastra*
341 B.C. Late Dynastic Period ends 332-30 B.C. Ptolmaic Period 332 B.C. Alexander the Great of Macedonia conquers Egypt	327-25 B.C. Alexander the Great of Macedonia invades India

Theatre of the Pre-Christian World,
800 B.C.-301 B.C.

CHINA   JAPAN

800 B.C.   Chou Dynasty continues

700 B.C.

660 B.C. 1st earthly emperor,
600 B.C.   Jimmu Tenno (legendary)

Kung Fu-tze (Confucius, c. 551-
479 B.C.)

500 B.C.

400 B.C.   c. 400-200 B.C. Jomon Period
Developing shamanistic practices   350 B.C.-250 A.D. Yayoi Period
Evidence of theatrical activity

332-295 B.C. *Ch'u Tz'u* anthology
contains *Nine Hymns*

Theatre of the Pre-Christian World, 800-301 B.C.

GREECE

800 B.C.

Age of Homer; *Iliad, Odyssey*

700 B.C.

600 B.C.

c. 600 B.C. Dithyrambic choruses
    established
c. 550 B.C. Thespis steps out of
    chorus to introduce speaker
534 B.C. Pisistratus introduces
    tragedy into City Dionysia Festival
Aeschylus (525-456 B.C.)
509-265 B.C. The Republic
c. 501 B.C. Satyr Plays added to
    City Dionysia Festival

500 B.C. Sophocles (c. 496-406 B.C.)
487 B.C. Comedy introduced into
    City Dionysia Festival
Euripides (c. 480-406 B.C.)
c. 471 B.C. Aeschylus introduces 2nd
    actor
c. 468 B.C. Sophocles introduces 3rd
    actor
462-429 B.C Age of Pericles
458 B.C. *Skene* (scene house) introduced
Aristophanes (c. 448-380 B.C.);
    Old Comedy
431-404 B.C. Peloponnesian Wars

400 B.C.

400-c. 320 B.C. Middle Comedy
399 B.C. Socrates tried and executed
Aristotle (384-322 B.C.); *Poetics*,
    335-323 B.C.
Menander (c. 342-c. 291 B.C.)
336-146 B.C. Hellenistic Age
336-300 B.C. New Comedy
c. 325 B.C. Theatre of Dionysus
    completed

ROME

753 B.C. Rome founded

Circus Maximus constructed
6th century B.C. Festivals

4th century Greek tragedies
    performed in Rome

EGYPT

• Herodotus, the Greek historian, was impressed with the mystery play of *Osiris* that he witnessed at a night performance. Some 500 years later, Plutarch attended a similar ritual play performed in a temple, indicating that the traditional Osiris mystery plays were performed even into the Christian era.

• Records show that Greek and Roman invaders introduced their dramas into Egypt and built theatres for performances.

INDIA

• In *Artha Sastra*, the Doctrine of Prosperity, Kautilya, a 4th century B.C. minister to an emperor, gives accounts of theatrical companies. Some modern scholars, however, question the book's authenticity, believing that parts were written in the 3rd or 4th centuries A.D.

• Alexander is known to have enjoyed actors and may have had theatrical troupes with him during his campaigns. Contact between Indian poets and Greek actors could have been a major influence upon the development of Sanskrit theatre.

CHINA

• Writings from the Chou Dynasty (1122-221 B.C.) suggest the growing performance activities of the shamans. The *Book of Rituals* describes costumes for dances; *Ch'u Tz'u*, an anthology of verse containing the *Nine Hymns* (332-295 B.C.), mentions costumes, face paintings, properties, dance, mime and song (perhaps in dialogue).

JAPAN

• Excavations of Yayoi Period (350 B.C.-250 A.D.) settlements have revealed clay miniatures of musical instruments and masks, as well as clay figures singing, dancing and playing musical instruments in ways that suggest modern celebrations of Shinto festivals, folk dances and skits.

GREECE   ─600 BC

• For reasons not clearly understood, a wild song (dithyramb) chanted by a chorus in honor of Dionysus, the Greek god of revelry, developed into a cheerfully grotesque satyr play (comedy) at about the same time that the Greek character qualities of intellectualism and a sense of humanity created a passionate tension that made the Greeks deeply appreciate a form of tragic drama. For most of the 5th century B.C., a tragic drama was written that persuades historians to claim Greece as the cradle of Western drama and theatre.

• Aeschylus' major plays include *The Suppliants* (490? B.C.), *Seven Against Thebes* (467 B.C.) and *The Oresteia* (458 B.C.). Among Sophocles' works are *Antigone* (c. 441 B.C.) and *Electra* (c. 418-416 B.C.). Euripides' plays include *Medea* (431 B.C.), *Hippolytus* (428 B.C.) and *The Bacchae* (406 B.C.). Aristophanes' (c. 448-380 B.C.) comedies best illustrate Old Greek Comedy with its three major parts: (1) the prologue, the parados, the agon; (2) the parabasis; and (3) the episodes. Among his major works are *The Clouds* (423 B.C.), *The Birds* (414 B.C.) and *Lysistrata* (411 B.C.).

• Affected by the downfall of Athens in 404 B.C., comedy changed. The extravagant wit of Aristophanes was abandoned for plays of intrigue in which the chorus might disappear, while the individual actor emphasized the realistic depiction of daily life, which was the aim of Middle Comedy.

• In his *Poetics* (c. 335-323 B.C.), Aristotle defined tragedy in terms of plot, character, thought, diction, melody and spectacle and considered it as positive and helpful to mankind in that it aroused pity and fear as a means of purging these emotions. Aristotle used Sophocles' *Oedipus Rex* (c. 430-425 B.C.) as a model, and of the three major writers of Greek tragedy, only Sophocles clearly illustrates Aristotle's theories. For Aeschylus, the tragic idea was catastrophe completed before the action of the play, thus revealing tragedy in a situation rather than in a character. More concerned with society than his predecessors, Euripides concentrated upon blind and irrational forces which unbalanced human nature to create disaster.

• New Comedy, of which only Menander's *Dyskolos* (c. 320 B.C.) is extant (of 98 known titles), continued the development away from the imaginative and fantastic, emphasized stock characters and turned serious in tone.

Theatre of the Pre-Christian World,
300 B.C.-0 B.C.

EGYPT	INDIA
300 B.C.	3rd century B.C. Composition of *Ramayama*, Valmiki *Therigatha*, a Buddhist text giving descriptions of string puppets
200 B.C.	Early evidence of shadow puppets 200 B.C.-200 A.D. Composition of *Natyasastra* by Bharata Composition of *Mahabharata* 140 B.C. Patanjali, *Mahabhasya*
100 B.C. Cleopatra (69-30 B.C.)	c. 100 B.C. Beginning of Sanskrit Drama 100 B.C.-100 A.D. Composition of *Bhagavad Gita*
30 B.C. Ptolmaic Period ends Egypt part of Roman Empire by 30 B.C. **0 B.C./A.D.** Birth of Christ	

Theatre of the Pre-Christian World,
300 B.C.-0 B.C.

SOUTHEAST ASIA AND CHINA	JAPAN AND KOREA
300 B.C.	
255 B.C. Chou Dynasty ends in China	
Entertainments, Court Jesters Jester Ming in China	
221-206 B.C. Chin Dynasty in China 1st Emperor of China, Chin Shih Huang-ti 214 B.C. Great Wall of China completed 206 B.C.-220 A.D. Han Dynasty in China	
200 B.C. Shamanism; folk drama and song in Southeast Asia 121 B.C. Legendary beginning of shadow puppetry in Java c. 121 B.C. Shamanistic use of shadow puppets in China 104 B.C. Imperial Office of Music established in China	Jomon Period ends in Japan Period of Three Kingdoms in Korea
100 B.C.	
	57 B.C.-935 A.D. Silla Period in Korea Korean folk ceremonies and shamanistic rites
0 B.C./A.D.	

Theatre of the Pre-Christian World, 300 B.C.-0 B.C.

GREECE

ROME

300 B.C.   Decline of New Comedy
277 B.C. Artists of Dionysus
    recognized

Gnaeus Naevius (270-201 B.C.), playwright
265 B.C. The Republic ends
264-241 B.C. 1st Punic Wars; Greek influence
    on Roman culture
Plautus (254-184 B.C.), playwright
Livius Andronicus (240-204 B.C.),
    translator of Greek tragedy into Latin
240 B.C. Comedy and tragedy added to
    Ludi Romani
Quintus Ennius (239-169 B.C.), playwright
238 B.C. Mimes at Ludi Florales

218-201 B.C. 2nd Punic Wars
200? B.C. Atellan Farce, boistrous skits
    performed by masked clowns

200 B.C.

146 B.C. Hellenistic age ends
Strong Roman influence on
    Greek theatre begins

Terence (c. 185-159 B.C.), playwright

Roscius (c. 126 B.C.-62 B.C.), popular actor

105 B.C. Gladiator fights become national
    celebration

100 B.C.

1st century B.C. Theatres built
    throughout Roman Empire
90 B.C. Vitruvius' *De Architectura*
c. 75 B.C. Theatre at Pompeii built
60 B.C. 1st Triumverate (Pompey, Crassus,
    and Julius Caesar)
55 B.C. 1st permanent stone theatre built
    in Rome
Horace (65-08 B.C.); *Ars Poetica*, 24-20 B.C.
43-28 B.C. 2nd Triumverate (Antony,
    Lepidus and Octavius)
27 B.C.-284 A.D. The Roman Empire

0 B.C./A.D.

Birth of Christ

Theatre of the Pre-Christian World, 300 B.C.-0 B.C.

INDIA

• Early Sanskrit writers (c. 100 B.C.) ascribe the origin of leather puppetry to Paravathi, the consort of Siva who dressed in a tiger skin. Because there is mention of *sutradhar*, or "string puller," in Sanskrit drama, it is believed that puppet shows were prevalent before Sanskrit dramas.

• Bharata's *Natyasastra*, the Indian book of dramaturgy composed sometime between 200 B.C. and 200 A.D., is comparable to Aristotle's *Poetics* but broader in scope. It covers acting, theatre architecture, costumery, make-up, properties, dance, music, play construction, theatre company management, audiences, drama competitions and the dramaturgical theories of *rasa* (sentiments) and *bhava* (psychological states).

• The *Mahabharata* is a wandering collection now divided into 18 books. The great battle of Kurukshetra, upon which the main story is based, presumably took place between 850 and 650 B.C. The two great families of the Kauravas and Pandavas are involved in innumerable stories traced through several generations.

• In *Mahabhasya*, a text of grammar, Patanjali does not mention *natya* (drama) specifically but indicates that action can be achieved through pantomime, recitation, song and dance.

• The *Bhagavad Gita*, "Song of the Lord," consisting of a dialogue between Krishna and Arjuna, is incorporated into the *Mahabharata*.

SOUTHEAST ASIA AND CHINA

• When the Chou Dynasty began to disintegrate in the mid 3rd century B.C., records show the existence of court jesters who entertained with jokes, songs and dances. The most famous was Jester Ming, a very tall man, who made much of his ability to imitate people with costumes, speech and gestures. Mock military spectacles were also popular, along with "horn butting" games and physical contests such as wrestling.

• The Han Dynasty (206 B.C.-220 A.D.) identifies the indigenous Chinese people and was an era of political and cultural diversity. Its most famous emperor, Wu Ti (140-87 B.C.), a believer in shamanism, furthered the practice of allowing shamans free access to the palace and a place in official government ceremonies.

• The diversity of the sea-faring people of the Malay archipelago is evident in their theatrical activity. Prior to the increasing influence of the Hindu, which dates from about 100 to 1500 A.D., Southeast Asians were predominantly animists who loved dancing, singing and playing. Evidence of pre-Christian era theatrical activity is completely lacking, but later written evidence of early folk traditions suggests that in many parts of

Southeast Asia (including Burma, Siam, Cambodia, Laos, Viet Nam, Malaysia, Sumatra, Bali, Java, Indonesia, Borneo and the Philippines) there were folk performances associated with the rites of animistic worship and, perhaps, in populous areas, the beginnings of a court supported theatre.

ROME

• Roman festivals (Ludi Romani) date back to the 6th century B.C., but there was no Roman drama until 240 B.C., when comedy and tragedy were added to the Ludi Romani, and even then it was much influenced by the Greeks. Probably all nine tragedies by Gnaeus Naevius (270-201 B.C.) were taken from Euripides. All 20 known titles by Quintus Ennius (239-169 B.C.) also suggest Euripides' work, as do plays by other Romans of this period. Unfortunately, no plays exist.

• Roman festivals grew in number as years passed, as did the number of days allotted to dramatic performances at regular festivals. In 200 B.C., for example, 11 days were allowed for the drama; 48 days were given to official dramatic entertainment by 78 B.C.

• Plautus (254-184 B.C.) was the most popular of all Roman comic writers, with plays such as *Amphitryon, The Rope* and *The Menaechmi.* Although dates of composition are unknown, presumably the plays were written between 205 and 184 B.C. The author of at least 45 plays, Plautus combined knowledge of his native Roman farce with an interest in Greek New Comedy, which he translated to Roman circumstance.

• In contrast to Plautus' robust farces, the comedies of Terence (c. 185-159 B.C.) emphasized character and language. Such plays as *The Eunuch* (161 B.C.), *Phormio* (161 B.C.) and *The Brothers* (160 B.C.) became models in the monasteries of the Middle Ages and the schools of the Renaissance for their style and their high moral tone.

• The Romans appear to have been born actors and achieved great skill in gesture and rhetorical delivery. Actors wore a variety of masks in tragedy and comedy but not in mime, where facial expression became an art. Both Cicero (106 B.C.-43 B.C.) and Quintillian (c. 35 A.D.-c. 95 A.D.) described acting, and popular actors were socially accepted and highly rewarded. Roscius (c. 126 B.C.-62 B.C.) is said to have acted 125 times one year and, when he died, left the equivalent of one million dollars.

• Horace's *Ars Poetica* (24-20 B.C.) stressed the rules that playwrights should follow. His advice that drama should both entertain and instruct influenced the work of future playwrights for centuries.

Theatre of First Six Centuries, A.D.

| EGYPT AND THE MIDDLE EAST | INDIA AND SOUTHEAST ASIA |

0   30 B.C.-390 A.D. Roman Period
     in Egypt
  Greek and Roman influence in
     theatre

100
                                      c. 100 A.D.-1500 A.D. Hindu
                                          influence throughout Malay
                                          Archipeligo
                                          c. 120-500 Golden Age of Indian
                                          Culture
                                          c. 2nd or 3rd century Bhasa, Indian

200
                                          playwright (13 plays);
                                          Vasavadatta Seen in a Dream

300
                                          320-647 Gupta Dynasty of India
                                          4th century King Shudraka, Indian
                                          playwright; *The Little Clay Cart*

   395-638 Byzantine Period   Late 4th-Early 5th century Kalidasa,
   Greek influence in theatre   Sanskrit playwright (3 plays);
                                          Shakuntala

400
   Turkic festivals include dances,
     mime and puppet shows

                                          Height of Sanskrit drama in India

500
   Mohammed (570-632)

Theatre of the First Six Centuries, A.D.

CHINA

0 Han to Sui Dynasty entertainments: circus acts, spectacles, court pageants, skits with scenery and properties

100

200

220 A.D. Han Dynasty ends
220-589 Period of Three Kingdoms
    and Six Dynasties
Emperor Ming Ti (reign 227-240)
    floods palace hall for water pageant
300 Non-Han Chinese contribute to theatre
The Stomping-Swaying Wife

386-534 Northern Wei Dynasty
Prince Lan-ling uses mask in battle
"No-Procession"

400

500

589-617 Sui Dynasty Spectacle
    pageants

JAPAN AND KOREA

Silla Period continues in
    Korea

Gi-ag, gum-mu and puppet
    theatre in Korea

250 A.D. Yayoi Period ends
    in Japan

494 A.D. Kingdom of Buyo ends
    in Korea
552 Buddhist influence comes to
    Japan from Korea
Legendary Japanese dance of
    Amano-Uzume-No-Mikoto
    (recorded in *Record of
    Ancient Matters,* 712)

Theatre of the First Six Centuries, A.D.

GREECE	ROME	MEDIEVAL EUROPE

0 227 B.C.-284 A.D. The Roman Empire: A period of "bread and circuses"

Greek theatre continues	Seneca (4 B.C.-65 A.D.),	
until after 500 A.D.	playwright (9 plays);	
Theatre of Dionysus	*Medea, Phaedra*	
undergoes changes to	52 Gigantic sea battle	
conform to Roman	spectacle on Fucine Lake	
standards	80 Colisseum opens	

c. 30-200 Romans build about 125 theatres and amphitheatres throughout Empire

100

200

c. 200 Tertullian,
On the Spectacles

284-476 The Roman Dominate

300

305-337 Constantine recognizes
Christianity
354 Theatrical entertainments
estimated to occupy 100
days

400

404 Gladitorial contests
abolished

5th century-7th or
8th century The *scop*
(storyteller)
flourishes

476 Fall of Rome; Dark
Ages begin

500

c. 500-c. 10th century
Period of traveling
performers

EGYPT AND THE MIDDLE EAST

• The Byzantine Empire contributed to theatre history mainly by preserving the manuscripts of the classical Greek playwrights.

• Folk traditions in 5th century Turkey indicate that at public festivals there were dances, mime shows and puppet shows (probably suggesting shamanistic rituals) and even crude sketches. One such sketch involves a Turk who goes to battle, leaving his wife at home, and returns for a forgotten amulet only to find a Chinese man attacking his wife. Enraged, he kills the man. Other folk skits, possibly originating in the Anatolian area, suggest that festivals took place to honor such gods as Dionysus (Greek), Attis (Phyrigian) and Osiris (Egyptian).

INDIA

• Sanskrit drama (c. 100 B.C.-1200 A.D.) reached its height in the 5th century and ceased to be effective theatre fare after the 12th century. Emphasizing the imitation of a situation rather than an action, Sanskrit dramas may be described according to the nine sentiments (*rasas*) and the nine psychological states (*bhavas*) and may vary in length from one to ten acts. Because all characters are described in detail in the *Natyasastra*, which also includes the rules for creating Sanskrit drama, the interest in story predominates, while the ending of a Sanskrit drama is always happy.

• The last centuries of the Gupta Dynasty (320-647), when southern India became a center of art and learning, closed the Golden Age of Indian Culture, which existed from about 120 to 500 A.D.

• The most enduring Sanskirt dramas are *The Little Clay Cart*, a social drama (*prakarana*) which deals with the life and affairs of a common man, and *Shakuntala*, a romantic story (*nataka*) of King Dushyanta and Shakuntala, their love, separation in consequence of a lost ring and their final meeting in heaven.

• Descriptions of the three types of Sanskrit playhouses -- triangular, square and oblong -- are given in the *Natyasastra*, along with the many conventions and gestures (*abhinaya*) in Sanskrit drama.

CHINA

• Theatre contributions of non-Han Chinese people included a comic sketch called *The Stomping-Swaying Wife,* about a drunken husband who habitually beat his wife, and the use of a mask by Prince Lan-ling of the Toba people (northern Wei Dynasty, 386-534), who wished to hide the effeminate features of his face in battle. The "No Procession," used by the Tai people to ward off evil spirits, dates from the Han Dynasty. Snake cultists among the Yüeh people employed ritual plays. Dynastic histories record tributes from tribes along the great trade routes that would have included a variety of performers.

• Spectacles from the Sui Dynasty (589-617) include a gigantic pageant involving 30,000 musicians and actors presented by Emperor Yang-Ti (605-617 reign) to impress Turkish ambassadors.

JAPAN AND KOREA

• Korea is best known for its mask drama which during the period of Silla (57 B.C.-935 A.D.) included the *gi-ag*, mask dance-dramas of importance to Buddhist believers, and sword dances or *gum-mu*. Evidence of puppet theatre suggests the influence of China, and dance movements indicate a knowledge of Japanese *gigaku* dance.

• The legendary 6th century dance of Uzume suggests the basic elements of all Japanese theatre: the supernatural, the erotic and dance. Because the sun-goddess, having hidden herself in a cave in a fit of pouting and thus thrown the world into darkness, could not be persuaded to show her face, Uzume danced around "pulling out the nipples of her breasts" and lowering her skirt. Laughter from those present caught the curiosity of the sun-goddess, who looked out, felt appeased and returned to her place in the heavens.

GREECE, ROME AND MEDIEVAL EUROPE

• During the Roman Empire gladitorial contests became increasingly popular, as well as wild aminal fights and spectacular sea battles involving thousands of people. Theatres seated thousands, too, as did the various circuses (last one built in Rome in 309). Actors, trained in speaking, singing and dancing, used masks and costumes.

• Rome's major writer of tragedy, Seneca (4 B.C.-65 A.D.), adapted all of his plays from Greek models. Although probably not performed in Rome, Seneca's work was a major influence during the Renaissance for its five-act structure, forensic speeches, moral interests, scenes of horror, theatrical conventions and single-minded heroes.

• The Dark Ages lasted from the Fall of Rome until about the year 1000. Storytellers, mimes and performers appeared in parts of Europe; festivals, which the church opposed, existed in Western Europe. Pagan rituals persisted.

World Theatre, 600-999

EGYPT AND THE MIDDLE EAST

600 Pre-Islamic processions,
carnival-like ceremonies and
dance-pantomimes by masked
performers
638 Byzantine Period ends
Mid 7th century Arabs bring
Islam to Persia

700

800

900

963 Early processions as
precursors of the *Ta'zieh*

1st descriptions of Shi'ite
Muharram rituals

INDIA AND SOUTHEAST ASIA

7th century King Harsha, Indian comic
playwright (3 plays); *Ratnavali*
7th century Mahendravekramarasman,
Indian playwright; *The Sport of
the Drunk Monk,* a farce

647 Gupta Dynasty ends in India
7th century Buddhism spreads to Tibet,
where *shanag* is accepted by Lamas

8th century Bhavabhuti, Indian playwright (3 plays)
8th (or 6th?) century Prince
Visakhadatta, Indian playwright

Decline of Sanskrit drama in India
9th century The Dramatic Sermon,
earliest form of theatre in Tibet

907 *Wayang kulit* shadow puppets
mentioned on stone inscription in
Java

CHINA

600
617 Sui Dynasty ends
618-906 T'ang Dynasty
Spectacles, pageants, farces
    sketches

700
714 Pear Garden Theatricals of
    Emperor Ming Huang (reign
    712-756)
"Hundred Entertainments"

800

900
906-1279 Sung Dynasty
Continued pageants, shadow
    puppetry
Beginnings of popular theatre

JAPAN AND KOREA

Gigaku mask dance and *bugaku*
    court dance of Japan

645-660 Beginning of Korean *kommu*
    sword dance
645-793 Nara Period in Japan
671-686 Wonkyo, priest of Silla, creates
    muaemu, court dance in Korea
Ch'oyongmu, Korean ritual court dance

793-1184 Heian Period in Japan
Kumhwan, acrobatic play of Korea
Soktok in Korea, similar to Japanese
    bugaku
Samye, Korean lion dance
Puppets introduced to Japan
9th-12th century *Kagura* dance in
    Japan, reanacting Uzume's dance

935 Silla Period ends in Korea
935-1392 Koryo Dynasty in Korea
Nanye, early mask drama in Korea

Ch'oyongmu performed as ritual dance
    and as festivity dance at Korean court
Period of "100 Shows" performed by
    Korean mimes, acrobats, jugglers,
    singers and dancers

World Theatre, 600-999

GREECE AND ROME	MEDIEVAL EUROPE
600 Dark Ages continue	Dark Ages continue *Scop* continues through 7th or 8th century Traveling performers continue into 10th century
700	
800	
900	
	c. 925 date of oldest extant Easter trope 965-975 earliest extant playlet (printed in *Regularis Concordia*, in England) 970 Hrosvitha, a nun in northern Germany, writes 6 plays modeled after Terence's comedies but with religious subject matter

EGYPT AND THE MIDDLE EAST

• The Turkic people, having established a large empire extending from Mongolia to the Black Sea, part of which came under Chinese sovereignty in the 7th century, may well be a link between Eastern and Western theatre. This link is suggested by the Arab annexation of ancient Sogdiana in the 7th century and subsequent contact of the Turkic people with the Persian Empire.

• The *Ta'zieh*, the passion play of the Shi'ite Muslim, is a dramatization of Hussein's martyrdom on the plains of Kerbela in 680. A 10th century account from Baghdad mentions people with faces painted black and with disheveled hair, beating their chests and moaning songs of lamentation for Hussein.

SOUTHEAST ASIA

• *Shanag*, a ritual dance performed at the end of the year to preserve that year from evil, uses costumes, masks and music to suggest a dispute between ancient local gods and demons.

• The Dramatic Sermon involves a prayer by Buddha, who is besieged by devils begging relief from the tortures of prayer until Buddha's moralizing sermon converts them to Buddhism.

• The flat leather puppets known as *wayang kulit* in Indonesia and Malaysia and *nang* in Siam, probably originated in India. Manipulated by a *dalang* (actor, singer, storyteller, playwright, leader of musical ensemble, shaman and teacher), the 2-3 foot puppets, articulated in their arms (one arm if Malaysian, two if Indonesian) and stuck into a banana log at the base of a 1 x 1.4 meter screen, are used to enact stories from the four popular cycles -- *Kuna, Arjuna, Rama, Pandawa*. A complete set might include 300-400 puppets, which may be described as either *alus* (refined) or *kesar* (coarse) and then categorized according to type: *juruk* (Rama-type), *kedelan* (aggressive), *gagah* (Bima-type), *gusen* (comic and stupid), *rakasasa* (evil). Performances run from 9 p.m. to 6 a.m. and are divided to present the three ages of man -- youth, the struggle, spiritual harmony. There are numerous pre-performance ceremonies and traditional conventions. On a mystical level the screen is heaven, the log is earth, the puppets are man and the *dalang* is god.

CHINA

• The T'ang Dynasty (618-906), known for its distinctive literary and theatrical accomplishments, had large-scale spectacles and pageants as well as farce sketches, such as *The Military Counselor*, which burlesqued the greed of an earlier official (330-44), and a dance with theatrical elements called *Po-t'ou*, about a man who killed a tiger. Emperor Ming Huang, famous for his Pear Garden Theatricals, reigned from 712-756.

• By the time of the T'ang Dynasty, the numerous and varied forms of entertainment -- both native and imported -- became known as the "Hundred Entertaiments": storytelling, dances, comic skits, animal and circus acts and a variety of puppet shows (string puppets, stick or rod puppets, puppets in small boats on water, puppets operated by explosive charges and live small children manipulated as puppets).

• During the Sung Dynasty there was increasing interest in the light-hearted skits dating from the T'ang Dynasty which would become the basis of the entertainments that brought thousands to the theatre districts in later years.

JAPAN AND KOREA

• *Gigaku* (skill music), a mask dance, was short-lived. Originally performed in India for Buddhist rites and imported to Japan from Korea, it had some ten varieties and was performed with enormous masks that covered the head.

• *Bugaku* (dance music), a court dance, is of two types: *left* dances imported from China, India and central Asia costumed in red; *right* dances imported from Korea and Manchuria costumed in green. Performed to classical court music, *bugaku* is structured in the three traditional parts associated with the *noh* drama: *jo,* a slow introduction; *ha,* a movement with a definite tempo; *kyu,* a swift movement and coda.

• During the 7th century three important dance forms developed containing some elements of theatre: the *kommu,* a mask sword dance concerned with the death of a young warrior; the *muaemu,* a dance in celebration of Buddhism; and the *ch'oyongmu,* a grotesque mask dance-drama based on the story of Ch'oyong, a son of the Dragon King of the East Sea.

• *Kagura* received the Japanese Emperor's patronage in the 16th century but thereafter declined until the 19th century.

• The *nanye,* the mask play of the early Koryo Dynasty (935-1392), employed horrifying masks to exorcise the evil spirits of the passing year. *Nanye* originated in the Chou Dynasty (1122 B.C.-249 B.C.) of China.

• The Korean mask dance-drama is divided into two parts: song and dance and a drama consisting of mime, action and dialogue. The masks are made of wood, paper and gourd and are painted different colors. The mask, worn only by men, has a wrapping at the back so that the entire head is covered. Common themes of Korean mask dance-dramas are ritual exorcisms, satire on apostate priests, conflict between spouses and the life of the poor.

MEDIEVAL EUROPE

• The *trope,* written for the Christian Easter service, is the oldest form of liturgical drama and is essentially an antiphonal elaboration in dialogue of the biblical text.

World Theatre, 1000-1299

THE MIDDLE EAST

1000 c. 1000 Unknown but ancient origin
of the *naqqal* -- Persian storyteller
Jesters in courts of Persian kings

Omar Khayyamm (c. 1050-1123)

1095-1099 1st Crusade, involving
European Christians, Seljuk Turks
and Egyptian Mamelukes
1100

1148 *The Alexiad* by Anna Comnena,
daughter of Emperor, describes
comic play performed at Seljuk
court
Shadow puppets popular in Egypt

1200

Attar (d. 1221), Persian poet,
writes of puppet theatre in
The Book of the Camel
1270 Mongols and Turks invade Persia
13th century *Meddahs* (panegyrists,
storytellers, solo comedians)
form guild at Baghdad
Late 13th century-1918 Ottoman
Empire

INDIA

Kutiyattam, a traditional form
of Sanskrit drama performed
in the temples of Kerala

Invasion of Islam (12th-15th
century) paralyzes Hindu
artistic activity
Gita Govinda, lyrical dramatic
Sanskrit work by Jayadeva
of the Krishna cult

Disappearance of Sanskrit
Drama

1221 1st Mongol invasions

1292-1293 Marco Polo visits
South India

SOUTHEAST ASIA

1000

    1005 *Hat cheo* (to sing-gesture),
    folk plays of social satire,
    performed in Viet Nam

1100

1200

    1293-1525 Javanese Empire of
    Majapahit, Golden Age of
    Arts and Literature

CHINA

Judge Pao (999-1062), magistrate
    whose career stimulates
    plays on theme of justice

1162 Abolishment of Imperial
    Office of Music encourages
    development of popular theatre
Development of "tile districts"
Imperial Training Center for Actors
Popularity of *tsa-ch'u,* a farce
    without a plot, and *yüan-pen,*
    comic entertainment
13th century Chi Chun-hsiang,
    playwright

Kuan Han-ch'ing (1224-1297),
    Father of Chinese Drama
1279-1368 Yüan (Mongol) Dynasty,
    The Golden Age of Chinese
    Theatre
Wang Shih-fu, playwright

Li Hsing-tao (13th or 14th century)
    playwright

World Theatre, 1000-1299

JAPAN AND KOREA

1000   Koryo Dynasty continues in Korea
9th-12th century *Kagura* dance
   in Japan
Heian Period court entertainments
   in Japan
c. 1023 1st reference to *dengaku*
Early 11th century Lady Murasaki,
   The Tale of Genji in Japan
c. 1060 *New Notes on Sarugaku*,
   attributed to Akihira Fujiwara
   (989-1066) in Japan

1100   Rise of professional actors in Korea
Book of Puppeteers by Oe Tadafusa
   in Japan

1150 *Dengaku* guilds begin in Japan

1184 Heian Period ends in Japan

1200

MEDIEVAL EUROPE

c. 1000 Dark Ages end
c. 1000 Liturgical plays incorporated
   into church services
c. 1000 *Beowulf*, oldest English epic

1066 Norman Conquest of Britain

The Mystery of Adam, religious
   play performed outside of church

1264 Feast of Corpus Christi
   established; celebrated widely
   by 1350
Hand and string puppets popular in
   Spain
1283 *The Play of Robin and
   Marion*, French folk play
Processions and street pageants
   popular

THE MIDDLE EAST

• Evidence of 11th century shadow puppets in Omar Khayyam's (c. 1050-1123) *Rubiayat* LXVIII:

> We are no other than a moving row
> Of magic shadow-shapes that come and go
>   Round with Sun-illumined lantern held
> In Midnight by the Master of the Show.

• Origins of shadow puppets are impossible to determine. The concept of the shadow play traveled from India or Southeast Asia and China, probably coming through Egypt, before arriving in Turkey. In both size and method of manipulation, the Middle Eastern shadow puppets suggest more ancestry in China than in Indonesia. Based on the Sufi Islamic doctrine that man is but a shadow manipulated by his Creator, Turkish shadow performances were designed to entertain and to provide religious experience. In Egypt, where shadow puppets were popular in the 12th century as lively and humorous entertainment, they eventually degenerated to be sufficiently bawdy that Sultan Jakmak not only banned performances but ordered that all properties and sets for shadow puppets be burned. That quality of bawdiness also became associated with the Turkish Karagoz, the main character of later Turkish shadow puppetry.

• The major puppet from Attar's *The Book of the Camel* (early 13th century) is called Pahlavan Kachal ("bald hero"), who, though more versatile and cultivated, compares well with Karagoz.

• *Meddahs*, apparently influenced by the Arab *naqqals*, enjoyed popular appeal as commentators (like Karagoz) on political and social events as early as the 9th century. Their stage is the coffee house.

INDIA

• *Kutiyattam* follows the criteria set forth in the *Natyasastra* and other stage manuals written in Kerala during the medieval period. The form had elaborate preliminaries and ritual observances and might take five to six nights to perform an act which could have been presented in less than one hour.

• The two broad categories of traditional Indian theatre were the temple-based forms and the social or community-based forms. They ranged from spectacles and pageants to light farces. Most plays were based on stories from the *Ramayana* and the *Mahabharata*. Imitating those who dramatized the Rama and Krishna cycles for use in the temples of northern India, the *Vaishnava* (worshipers of Vishnu) monasteries in eastern India produced lyric drama called *ankia nat*. Similar dance-dramas developed later in temples elsewhere in India.

CHINA

• During the Sung Dynasty (906-1276), the "Official Copies of Miscellaneous Plays" listed 280 play titles, which included the entertainments, farces and variety sketches popular in the expanding "tile districts." These entertainment centers, which might hold as many as fifty theatres, were enormously popular. Hangchow had seventeen amusement districts inside and outside the city, where theatres identified as "Lotus Tent" or "Peony Tent" would entertain thousands. Supporting the districts were the Imperial Training Center for Actors and an improving quality of sketches such as *Sun, The Little Butcher* or *Chang Shieh, The First-Class Graduate.*

• Chi Chun-hsiang's (13th century) *The Orphan of the Family Chao* is the first Chinese play to be made known to the Western world through adaptations by Voltaire and Arthur Murphy. Kuan Han-ch'ing (1224-1297) wrote 63 plays of which 17 are extant, including *Injustice to Tou Ngo, Moon-Prayer Pavilion* and *Slicing Fish*. Wang Shih-fu's (late 1200's) *The Romance of the Western Chamber* is a long romantic play in more than 20 acts. Li Hsing-tao's (13th or 14th century) popular court drama of *The Chalk Circle* stimulated Bertolt Brecht to write *The Caucasian Chalk Circle* in 1944.

JAPAN

• *Dengaku* Field Dances, involving acrobatics and juggling, were performed at harvest festivals. After gaining the patronage of Shinto shrines and becoming popular as a social dance, *dengaku* eventually added mime to become *dengaku-no-noh*.

• *Sarugaku* Mimes ("monkey music"), originally coarse and vulgar comedy, were adapted and acted by Buddhist priests. Eventually they became *sarugaku-no-noh*.

MEDIEVAL EUROPE

• Liturgical plays required one or more "mansions" (or scenic structures) in various locations within the church. Outside the church vernacular religious plays made greater staging demands in performances that spread throughout western Europe.

• Conceived by Pope Urban IV, the Festival of Corpus Christi celebrated the redemptive power of Christianity and the union of man and God through the life and resurrection of Christ. By attempting to bring the church closer to the common people, the Festival or Feast encouraged a celebratory participation that led to the creation of drama and theatre.

World Theatre, 1300-1499

THE MIDDLE EAST	INDIA

1300 Ottoman Empire continues

1400 Variety of popular entertainments and court jesters
Growing popularity of shadow puppets
1407 Byzantine emperor visits Sultan Beyazit, records performances of musicians, singers, dancers and actors during 15th and 16th centuries
1451 Sultan Jakmak of Egypt bans shadow theatre

Medieval Period (10th-16th centuries) considered the Dark Ages of Indian Theatre
Ramalila and *Raslila*, Rama and Krishna cycle plays, evolve in temples of Northern India

World Theatre, 1300-1499

SOUTHEAST ASIA

1300 *Wayang kulit* puppets develop
  to present form
Islamic influence begins
Wayang orang, Javanese dance-
  drama, performed in royal courts
Composition of Panji cycle stories
Khon, mask dance-drama, in royal
  courts of Siam, *Ayudhia* Period
  (1350-1767)
Lakon jatri, oldest form of Siamese
  theatre comes to Siamese capital
1353 Khmer court introduces court
  dances, the Jataka stories, to
  Laos
1391 1st Dali Lama of Tibet

1400

1431 Traditional date for beginning
  of Siamese classical dance
1458 1st mention in Siamese records
  of *nang yai,* shadow puppets cut
  to represent scenes without
  articulated parts

CHINA

"Country Cousin at the Theatre,"
  (13th or 14th century), poem,
  by Tu Shan-fu
Kao Ming (1310-1380), playwright
1324 Mural depicts theatrical
  production
Ch'uan ch'i, popular form of
  southern Chinese drama

1368 Yüan (Mongol) Dynasty ends
1368-1644 Ming Dynasty
Imperial Office of Music
  reestablished
Government builds theatres
1398 *The Sounds of Universal
  Harmony* lists 12 traditional
  categories of drama

World Theatre, 1300-1499

JAPAN AND KOREA

1300   Early 14th century Existence of
musical storytelling in Japan,
foreshadowing *bunraku* and
kabuki theatres
Yi Saek (1328-1396) composer of
sandae chapkuk in Korea
Kannami Kiyotsugu (1333-1384),
Japanese *sarugaku* actor

Zeami Motokiyo (1363-1444), *noh*
playwright in Japan
Beginnings of *noh* drama in Japan
1392 Koryo Dynasty ends in Korea
1392-1910 Yi Dynasty in Korea
Sande-dogam plays in Korea
Nanye continues in Korea
1400

Kyogen becomes a recognized
theatrical form by end of 15th
century in Japan

MEDIEVAL EUROPE

Height of Liturgical Drama
c. 1300-c. 1650 Italian Renaissance
c. 1302 Dante's *The Divine Comedy*
c. 1315 Albertino Mussato's
Eccerinus, earliest Italian
tragedy, modeled after Seneca

c. 1375 *The Second Shepherd's
Play,* English cycle play
c. 1387 Chaucer's *The Canterbury Tales*

c. 1425 *The Castle of Perseverance,*
English Morality Play
1429 Plautus' plays rediscovered
in Italy
c. 1450 Gutenberg invents moveable type
c. 1470 *Pierre Patelin,* French farce
c. 1473 *Robin Hood and the Sheriff
of Nottingham,* English play
1481 Spanish Inquisition
1485 Italian government supports
playwrights
1486 Vitruvius' treatise on Roman
architecture, *De Arcketectura,*
printed
1491-1500 1st play written in Spanish
for secular audience
1492 Columbus crosses Atlantic Ocean
c. 1495 *Everyman,* English
Morality Play
1495 *Everyman,* Dutch Morality Play
1499 *The Comedy of Calisto and
Melibea* early Spanish secular
drama

SOUTHEAST ASIA

• The *khon* evolved from the shadow plays, and actors copied the movements of the puppets. All actors, except those representing buffoons or impersonating women, wore masks. Gestures replaced language, although narration and dialogue were supplied in a singing voice by a person in the background.

• The *lakon jatri* evolved from Indian dance and Buddhist subject matter. Dancers performed acrobatic movements, and a troupe consisted of three actors, only men -- hero, female impersonator and clown/ogre/animal -- plus singers and musicians.

CHINA

• "Country Cousin at the Theatre" provides information on the sketches, actors and theatre of the Yüan period (1279-1368). A mural from the Yüan period shows the tradtional bare rectagonal stage which is still associated with Chinese theatre, a theatre completely lacking in a sense of realism. Identified by costume and face painting, the actors and actresses assumed one of five major character roles: *sheng* (hero), *tan* (female), *ching* (villain), *ch'ou* (comic) and *mo* (secondary role). Yüan Dynasty plays, characterized as civil or military, were generally divided into a "peg" or introduction and four acts, with the heart of the drama in the third act and calm restored in the final act. In general, the act divisions were established by editors from the later Ming Dynasty (1368-1644).

• Kao Ming's (1310-1380) *Lute Song* is a romantic drama representing the popular southern Chinese form of *ch'uan ch'i*.

• Early in the Ming period (1368-1644), the Imperial Office of Music was reestablished, and theatre troupes became associated with the emperor's court, wealthy families or the professional world of touring theatre.

JAPAN AND KOREA

• *Sandae chapkuk*, composed by Yi Saek (1328-1396) -- a spectacle show at the end of the Koryo period including *ch'oyongmu*, acrobatic feats, stilt walking, song, mime and dance -- delighted audiences largely through sensual excitement.

• *Noh* appeared as the mime of *sarugaku* and the dance of *dengaku* were combined through the acting of Kannami Kiyotsugu (1333-1384), a *sarugaku* actor who incorporated the elements of Zen Buddhism into his art.

• Zeami Motokiyo (1363-1444), the son of Kannami, was the playwright and theorist to bring perfection to the *noh* theatre. Zeami wrote more than 100 plays and three treatises.

Again, Zen Buddhism was a strong influence, revealed in Zeami's concept of *yugen*, sometimes explained as "graceful elegance," the technique of presenting the profundity of sentiment, and *monomane*, a theory of realism and a technique of imitation. *Noh*, meaning "to be able," is classified under five types of plays -- god, man, woman, mad people, demons -- and is accompanied by a chorus and musicians. The major actors are the *shite* (principal character) and *waki* (secondary), whose performances are measured by "the third quality of *noh*," flower or *hana*, which Zeami described as "bewitching the audience." Costumes are rich and impressive; properties are few. The stage is composed of a *hashigakari* (flower path) and the major acting area.

• *Nanye,* at first a religious spectacle to expel devils, changed into spectacles of dramatic performance. Records indicate that at the beginning of the 12th century this change gave rise to professional actors.

• The Yi Dynasty (1392-1910) retained interest in both *sandae chapkuk,* which it used extensively, and *nanye.*

• *Sande-dogam,* a combination of all past mask dramas, developed during the Yi Dynasty and involved a criticism of priests and upper-class society.

• *Kyogen* ("mad words"), a recognized theatrical form by the end of the 15th century, emphasized the early comic ideals of the *sarugaku.* In contrast to the philosophical *noh* drama, *kyogen* was meant to "kindle the mind to laughter." It dealt with the ordinary world of greed, drunkenness and coarse perversity. These short farces, employing only two or three common characters, almost always without music or chorus, were performed by actors trained in only this professional form which provided a contrasting atmosphere to the demanding seriousness of the *noh.*

MEDIEVAL EUROPE

• Medieval theatre was most prominent from 1350 to 1550. Mystery or cycle plays, such as the English Wakefield Cycle (32 plays) with *The Second Shepherd's Play*, date from about 1375. One manner of staging a cycle play was on a "pageant wagon." Fixed stages of the time suggest greater scenic complexity, special effects and the use of music.

• The Morality Play was a secular reaction to religious drama, popular in England and on the Continent. As a distinct form, it flourished between 1400 and 1550.

• In addition to liturgical plays performed across Europe during this period, there were also farces commenting on society and occasional skits for banquets, tableaux, and festival parades.

World Theatre, 1500-1649

THE MIDDLE EAST

INDIA

1500 Ottoman Empire continues
1499-1739 Safavid Dynasty of Iran
Period of elaborate parades during
  month of Muharram
1517-1798 Turkish domination of
  Egypt

1526 Mogul Empire founded by
  Beber, a Moslem; consolidated
  by Akbar

1550 Probable introduction of *bazi*
  (play or sketch) by Kal Enâyat,
  clown in court of Shah Abbâs
  (reign 1587-1628) of Iran

1550 Period of developing
  kathakali in state of
  Kerala

1585 Festival entertainments in
  in Turkey for circumcision
  of Mehned, sultan's son

1600

Dark Ages of Indian Theatre end
1612 British East India Company
  establishes trading station
  at Surat

1617-1623 *Meddahs* perform in
  court of Turkey's Sultan
  Mustapha I

1630-1648 Building of Taj Mahal

Mid 17th century Specific mention of
  karagoz puppet theatre in Turkey
Motreb (musicians and dancers) in
  traveling troupes in Iran

World Theatre, 1500-1649

SOUTHEAST ASIA

1500 Hindu influence declines in
Malay archipeligo

1525 Invasion of Islam in Java;
aristocrats and gurus flee
to Bali

1550

Late 16th century *Wayang gedog*
shadow puppets introduced
to Java
Wayang golek doll puppets
Wayang beber picture scrolls
Wayang topeng mask dance

1600
1602 Dutch East India Company
established in Indonesia

CHINA

Hsu Wei (1521-1593), playwright
of *tsa ch'u* form

Mid 16th century Popularity of
ch'uan ch'i

1550 Rise of *k'un ch'u*
Liang Ch'en-yu (1520-1580),
k'un ch'u playwright
T'ang Hsien-tsu (1550-1616),
k'un ch'u playwright

1644 Ming Dynasty ends
1644-1911 Ching (Manchu)
Dynasty

World Theatre, 1500-1649

JAPAN

1500

1550

1560 Introduction of the *samisen* to Japan affects the puppet theatre

1586 O'Kuni performs a dance including religious and erotic characteristics
1596-1610 Introduction of *joruri* chanters and storytellers
1600 Decline of *kagura*
1603-1867 Tokugawa Period, last of the shogunates
1616 7 licensed *pleasure woman's kabuki* theatres in Tokyo
1617 Existence of *young men's kabuki* and homosexual activity
1629 *Pleasure woman's kabuki* banned

1642 Sakon Murayama, 1st female interpreter (*onnagata* role)
1648 Homosexuality (*shudo*) banned

ITALY

Renaissance continues
1508 *The Casket* by Lodovico Ariosto (1474-1533), 1st vernacular drama
c. 1513-15?0 *Mandragola*, comedy by Niccolo Machiavelli (1469-1527)
1515 *Sofonisba* by Giangiorgio Trissino (1478-1550), 1st important tragedy
1541 *Obecche* by Gianbattista Cinthio (1504-1573), 1st tragedy produced
1545 *Architettura* by Sebastiano Serlio (1475-1554), 1st work to devote a section to theatre
1548 1st commentary on Aristotle's *Poetics*
c. 1550 1st reliable records of *commedia dell'arte*
c. 1569 *Commedia dell'arte* company of I Gelosi formed

1584 Teatro Olimpico completed

1618 Teatro Farnese opens
1638 *Manual for Constructing Theatrical Scenes and Machines* by Nicola Sabbattini (1574-1654)
1641-1645 Giacomo Torelli (1608-1678) develops pole-and-chariot system

World Theatre, 1500-1649

SPAIN

1500 Development of the *auto sacramentale*
Juan del Encina (1469-1529), founder of Spanish drama
Lope de Rueda (c. 1510-c. 1565), 1st important playwright and performer

Miguel de Cervantes (1547-1616), author of *Don Quixote* and about 36 plays
1550 1550-1650 Golden Age of Spanish Theatre
Juan de la Cueva (1550-1610), playwright
Lope de Vega (1562-1635), author of 450-2000 plays

1579 Corral de la Cruz, Spain's 1st permanent theatre, opens
1583 Corral del Principe opens
1588 English defeat Spanish Armada

1600 Pedro Calderón de la Baca (1600-1681), author of about 200 plays
1604 *Entertaining Journey* by Rojas Villandrando tells of actors' lives
c. 1614 *The Sheep Well* by Lope de Vega
c. 1636 *Life Is a Dream* by Calderón

1640 Coliseo, court theatre with proscenium arch, opens

1646-1651 *Corrales* (public theatres) closed

FRANCE

16th century Transitional period in theatre

1518 Confrérie de la Passion given monolopy among Paris theatres

1548 Paris Parliament bans sacred drama (affects only Ile de France)
1548 Hôtel de Bourgogne, public theatre, opens in Paris
1549 La Pléiade proposes that comedies and tragedies be written in French

Alexandre Hardy (c. 1572-1632), 1st professional playwright, about 500 plays

1598 The King's Players founded by Valleran le Comte (d. 1613)
Pierre Corneille (1606-1684), playwright

1629 French Academy founded
1636 *Le Cid* by Corneille
1637 *Discourse on Method* by René Descartes (1596-1650)
1641 Growing Italianate influence on French theatre
1645 Cardinal Mazarin brings Giacomo Torelli to Paris

World Theatre, 1500-1649

ENGLAND

1500

c. 1520 *The Foure PP*, farce, by
   John Heywood (c. 1497-c. 1589)
1533 Birth of Elizabeth I (reign
   1558-1603)

1550   1550/3 *Ralph Roister Doister*
   by Nicholas Udall (1505-1556)
1562 *Gorborduc*, 1st tragedy, by Thomas
   Norton and Thomas Sackville
1572 Actors legally recognized
1574 Master of Revels to examine plays
   and license theatre companies
1574 Earl of Leicester's Men licensed
1576 Blackfriars, 1st private theatre
Playwrights: Thomas Kyd (1558-1594),
   William Shakespeare (1564-1616),
   Christopher Marlowe (1564-1593),
   Ben Jonson (1572-1637)
1599 Globe Theatre built
1600   c. 1610 Playwrights' emphasis changes
1611 King James Bible
1613/14 *The Duchess of Malfi*
   by John Webster (c. 1580-c. 1630)
1620 Inigo Jones (1573-1652), stage
   designer, flourishes
1634 *The Triumph of Love* , court
   masque, by James Shirley (1596-
   1666)
1642 Parliament closes theatres
1644 *Areopagitica* by John Milton
   (1608-1674)
1649 Charles I beheaded

CENTRAL AND NORTHERN EUROPE

16th century Jesuit drama in Hungary
1509 *Maria Hoedeken,* Dutch miracle
   play, by Cornelius Everaert (1485-
   1556)

1539 *Hecastus,* Dutch adaptation of
   Everyman, by Georgius Macropedius
   (1486-1558)
1540 *Bassarus*, Dutch comedy, by
   Guilelmus Gnaphaeus (1493-1568)
Hans Sachs (1494-1576), German
   playwright
1558 *Magyar Elektra* by Peter Bomemisya
   (1535-1584), Hungarian playwright
1561 Colorful parade in Antwerp suggests
   popularity of dramatic contests

1578 *The Dismissal of the Grecian
   Envoys,* Polish secular play, by
   Jan Kochanowski (1530-1584)
1590's English troupes tour Germany
Hieronymous Justesen Ranch (1534-1607),
   Finnish author of school comedies
German Shrovetide and carnival plays
1616-1648 30 Years War in Germany
1616 Jacob Grein and his English
   Comedians in Poland
1633 Oberammergau Passion Play begins
Playwrights: Johannes Messenius (1579-
   1630), Jacobus Chronander (d. 1694),
   Sweden; Joost van den Vondel (1587-
   1679), Netherlands
1637 1st permanent theatre in Warsaw
1646 *Cardenio and Celinda,* German
   bourgeois tragedy, by Andreas
   Gryphius (1616-1664)

THE NEW WORLD

1500

1550

1567 2 comedies performed at Spanish
        mission in Tequesta, Florida

1570's Corpus Christi celebrations
        in Cuba

1590 Comedies and interludes staged
        in Cuba
1598 Performance of comedy by Marcos
        Farfán north of Rio Grande River
        in New Mexico

1600

1606 *The Theatre of Neptune in
        New France* by Marc Lescarbot
        (1570/75-1634?) at Port Royal in
        Nova Scotia
1607 Jamestown, Virginia, founded
1620 Pilgrims land at Plymouth Rock
1627 Mexico City's Coliseo theatre built
1636 Harvard College founded

THE MIDDLE EAST

• Under the Safavid monarchs (1499-1739) the Shi'ite form of Islam became the state religion of Iran, and the processional pageants mourning the fate of the martyrs during the month of Muharram became far more elaborate, with mounted celebrants and gruesome sights showing bloody wounds and missing limbs. Funereal music accompanied the performers.

• The sketches of Enâyat the Bald had such titles as *The Eye Healing* and *The Canvas Shop*. Other Ottoman Empire entertainments included dances, circus acts, puppetry, pageant carts, processions, tournaments and live actors.

• *Karagoz* was one of a number of shadow theatre performances played by Turkish mimes of the Ottoman Empire, perhaps as early as the 14th century. Evliya Chelebi's *Narrative Travels in Europe, Asia, and Africa* (1670) mentions rope artists, tumblers, jugglers, dancers, animal trainers, singers, clowns, athletes, storytellers, musicians, players with fire and sword and shadow puppet players. In his work, Chelebi identifies *karagoz* as a performance distinct from the generic type of shadow puppet theatre.

• The principal figures in a *karagoz* shadow puppet play, Karagoz and Hacivat, are articulated at the waist, legs and knees. Other puppets and puppet shows reflect the broad scope of the Ottoman Empire, the various ethnic people, their lives and problems. Shadow plays are divided into five parts: the introduction, the *muhaddeme* in which Hacivat recites prayers, the *muhavere* which consists of a debate between Karagoz and Hacivat, the *fasel* or plot and the epilogue. Karagoz, the hunchback spokesman for the common man, is a colorful storyteller and witty clown who can say and do anything, generally without censorship.

• *Motreb* performers visited the houses of the rich to sing comic songs and present romantic sketches. They employed *taqlid* (imitation), buffoonery and lewd actions.

INDIA

• The invasion of India by foreign peoples with different cultures and religious beliefs would affect India's theatre, but neither Islam nor Christianity would completely eliminate traditional Hindu theatre practices.

• The *Natyasastra* divides dance into three groups: *natya* (dance-dramas that tell a story), *nritya* (fusions of song and dance) and *nritta* (pure rhythmic dances). In the state of Kerala in southwest India hundreds of dances and dance-dramas were performed, their dates of origin obscured by time.

• One of the most popular of the dance-dramas, *kathakali*, attained a certain form with eight known dance-dramas based on stories from the *Ramayana* and recorded in the mid 16th century. In *kathakali* the dialogue is sung by reciters to the accompaniment of rhythmic instruments as actors in elaborate face painting, head gear and costumes interpret the story thought gesture and movement involving intricate foot and hand movements as well as incredible eye, eyebrow, cheek and lip activity. Types of characters include the *pacca* (kingly), *katti* (demonic), *tati* (red-bearded) and *kari* (demoness). Elaborate rituals precede performances in which the stories come from both the *Ramayana* and the *Mahabharata*.

• Other dances and dance-dramas include the *kathak* from north India and the *yakshagana*, a folk dance-drama from Kerala.

SOUTHEAST ASIA

• In Southeast Asia *wayang* means play. *Wayang gedog* refers to shadow puppets that tell stories from the Panji cycle. *Wayang golek* are doll puppets that tell stories of Islamic heroes. *Wayang beber* are paper scroll plays in which the stories are revealed through the unrolling of long paper picture scrolls. *Wayang topeng* is a mask dance in which Panji cycle stories are performed at courts or in villages.

CHINA

• Hsu Wei (1521-1593), the author of *The Four Shrieks of a Monkey*, was the most famous writer of *tsa ch'u*, which was practically abandoned by mid 16th century for the more popular *ch'uan ch'i*, the long romantic drama from southern China, illustrated by *The Romance of the Hairpin* by Li Ching-yun.

• *K'un ch'u* is the only lasting theatrical contribution of the Ming Dynasty (1368-1644). Combining the musical styles of *yi-yang* (drums, gongs and cymbals) and *hai-yen* (lute and moon guitar), *k'un ch'u* creates a smooth, sensuous and gentle style which supported the literary quality of the dramatic form. Some 77 playwrights wrote more than 150 *k'un ch'u* operas.

• Liang Ch'en-yu (1520-1580) is known for *Washing Gauze*, a romantic story from ancient China. T'ang Hsien-tsu (1550-1616) is remembered for *The Peony Pavilion*, a long romantic play in 55 scenes which would have taken several days to perform. Costumes, acting techniques, literary value and the lack of military attitudes distinguished the *k'un ch'u*.

JAPAN

• Early chanting/storytelling had its effect upon the doll or puppet theatre. The chanters took their name -- *joruri* -- from the 16th century ballad *The Tale of Princess Joruri*.

• *Kabuki* ("song-dance-skill") made its hesitant appearance during the early 17th century. Its erotic beginnings with O'Kuni's dance contributed to the problems it faced, and it would not become established as a dramatic form until the late 17th century, when *men's kabuki* (*yaro*) began to deemphasize the sexual and physical aspects and develop the art form which is recognized in modern times.

ITALY

• Few significant plays were written during this period, but a renewed if restrictive interest in Aristotle's *Poetics* left its mark for two centuries, and a new form of theatre art appeared with the *commedia dell'arte*. The *Poetics* was published by Robertello in 1548. Later commentators included Antonio Minturno (d. 1574), Julius Caesar Scaliger (1498-1558) and Lodovico Castelvetro (1501-1571).

• Through its numerous innovations in theatre architecture and design, the Italian Renaissance, stretching from the early 14th century to about 1650, illustrates the rebirth of the theatrical art form. Andrea Palladio (1518-1580) designed the Teatro Olimpico (1584), which was completed by Vincenzo Scamozzi (1552-1616). Giovan Battista Aleotti (1546-1636) designed the Teatro Farnese (1618).

• Although improvisation has probably been a part of theatrical performance since early shamanistic practice, the "comedy of professional artists" -- *commedia dell'arte* -- was a distinctive contribution to theatrical art. With its basic scenario outline rather than a written text, standard comic business called *lazzi* and stock characters such as Pantalone the lecherous miser, Dottore the braggart soldier, and Harlequin -- or Arlecchino -- the sly servant, the form was tremendously popular during the Italian Renaissance and has influenced theatre performance ever since.

SPAIN

• Combining the characteristics of the morality and mystery plays, the *autos sacramentales* developed with the increased interest in the Corpus Christi festivals to celebrate the power of the church, its sacraments and its dogma.

• The Golden Age of Spanish Theatre dates from about 1550 to 1650, but the plays of the Golden Age were produced until well after mid 18th century. During its height, the Golden Age was as vital as the theatre of Elizabethan England with which it is often favorably compared. After the death of Calderón in 1681 a serious decline in Spanish drama occurred.

• Lope de Vega (1562-1635), one of the two playwrights who dominated Spain's Golden Age, created the dramatic formula for the 17th century *comedia*. An extremely prolific playwright whose single objective was to please audiences, a concept he developed in *The New Art of Playwriting* (c. 1609), Lope wrote about 2000 plays spanning every genre. Among his numerous disciples was Gabriel Telley (Tirso de Molina, 1584-1628).

• Pedro Calderón de la Baca (1600-1681), considered Spain's foremost playwright, refined Lope's formula for the *comedia* and developed a new type of *auto sacramentale* which became so popular that none but his were presented after 1649. He wrote 111 secular plays and 70 *autos sacramentales*. For court entertainments, Calderón wrote poetic musical dramas. Among his greatest disciples were Agustin de Moreto y Cabaña (1618-1669) and Francisco de Rojas Zorrilla (1607-1648).

FRANCE

• Religious wars partially explain the 16th century as a transitional period in French theatre. Greek/Latin translations affected the writing of tragedy , and Italy influenced both tragedy and comedy as well as theatre scenic design and architecture. Additionally, a group of young poets and scholars, La Pléiade, seemed determined to have plays written in the French language. By the end of the 16th century the provincial and popular theatre had virtually disappeared, as theatre activity became concentrated in Paris, where Villeran le Comte (d. 1613) became the first important theatrical manager.

• Pierre Corneille (1606-1684), the first of the great French neoclassical playwrights, wrote 34 plays in a wide variety of genres.

ENGLAND

• As theatrically rich as the Italian Renaissance, the essential quality of the English Renaissance lies in its drama -- from the variety of farce, tragedy and tragi-comedy of the pre-Shakespearean era, through the brilliant plays of Marlowe, Shakespeare and Ben Jonson, to the contributions of Jacobean and Carolinian playwrights. Roman models were, at first, popular, as were the rules of Horace and the conventions of the Italian stage which, with the production concepts of the medieval theatre, created a stage ready for Shakespeare. Pre-Shakespearean plays include *Gammer Gurton's Needle* (1552-1563), a farce, probably by William Stevenson (d. 1575), Thomas Kyd's (1558-1594) *The Spanish Tragedy* (c. 1587) and *Dr. Faustus* (c. 1588) by Christopher Marlowe (1564-1593).

• Ben Jonson (1572-1637) appealed to court audiences, for whom he wrote masques, and to later audiences with his comedies, such as *Volpone* (1606). Among other playwrights of this period were John Marston (1576-1634), Thomas Dekker (c. 1572-c. 1632), Thomas Heywood (c. 1574-1641), Thomas Middleton (1580-1627) and Cyril Tourneur (1579/80- 1625/ 26). Among the playwrights whose work exemplified the shift of emphasis from a probing analysis of the human situation to the production of simple entertainment, shown after 1610 in both choice of subject matter and theatrical contrivances, were John Fletcher (1579-1625) and Francis Beaumont (c. 1584-1616) with some 50 plays in collaboration, Philip Massinger

(1583-1639/40), John Webster (c. 1580-c. 1630) and John Ford (1586-c. 1639). The works of James Shirley (1596-1666) suggest the extravagant court masques given at the Inns of Court.

• Opportunity for playwrights was strengthened by the emergence of a public theatre, increasingly favorable conditions for actors, growing patronage from court and private sources and the encouragement of theatre through royal decrees. The imaginative staging techniques added to the popularity of a theatre in which actors could achieve renoun.

CENTRAL AND NORTHERN EUROPE

• German Jesuit plays dramatized the lives of saints. The most popular of these plays were written by Jacob Bidermann (1576-1639).

• Hans Sachs (1494-1576) was a prolific German playwright, the author of 63 tragedies, 64 comedies, 85 *fastnachtsspiele* and some 1700 farces. His fame rests mainly on his Shrovetide plays, which satirize the follies of the world. His popular titles include *The Pregnant Peasant* (published 1544) and *The Stolen Shrovetide Hen* (published 1550).

• In 1600 Shrovetide and carnival plays were usually one-act skits presenting themes and scenes from burgher life.

• Swedish playwright Johannes Messenius (1579-1630) wrote a cycle of six plays on Swedish legends and history. Another Swede, Jacob Chronander (d. 1694), wrote such comedies as *Rise Up* (1647) and *Wooing Talk* (1649). Dutch playwright Joost van den Vondel (1587-1679) wrote 32 plays, either imitating the work of Plautus and Terence or based on biblical or historical subjects.

THE NEW WORLD

• The beginnings of recognized theatre in the Americas were stimulated by explorers and missionaries. The activity in Cuba reflected the European interest in liturgical drama as well as subsequent secular interests in comedy. Of the two comedies performed in Tequesta, Florida, under the direction of a lay brother named Francisco de Villareal, one dealt with the war between man and the world, the flesh and the devil.

• Captain Marcos Farfán de los Godos was in the process of taking possession of New Mexico "for God and the King of Spain" when he decided to compose and perform a play about his conquest (1598).

• Marc Lescarbot (1570/75-1634?) was a French lawyer, historian, poet, playwright and traveler who sailed with Samuel Champlain and Jean de Biencourt to explore the northern regions which he called Canada.

World Theatre, 1650-1749

THE MIDDLE EAST

1650 Ottoman Empire continues
Karagoz continues

1659 Court of Turkish Sultan
Haialdji: artist of shadow
theatre

1671-75 Chardin, French
traveler in Persia, notes
acrobats, conjurers, "lewd"
skits and 3-hour plays with
actors wearing masks

1690's European travelers collect
materials and stories of Turkish
meddahs
1700 c. 1710 Shi'ite clergy forbids
appearance of women as dancers
or players
c. 1710 Turkish theatre troupes
perform in teahouses and
wealthy homes

1737 Safavid Dynasty ends
in Iran

INDIA AND SOUTHEAST ASIA

17th century Spanish Catholic
priests create *moro-moro* drama
in Philippines
17th century Mystery plays in Tibet
Popular folk theatre in India
expands

1720-1911 Manchu (Chinese) over-
lordship in Tibet
1744-1748 1st Anglo-French War
involves division of Asia
c. 1749 *Lakon nai* dance-dramas
adapted from *lakon nok* for
Siamese courts

World Theatre, 1650-1749

CHINA

1650 Ching (Manchu) Dynasty continues
Hung Sheng (1645-1704), playwright
K'ung Shang-jen (1648-1718),
playwright

1671 Theatres forbidden in the
Inner City of Peking

1700

1724 Officials barred by law
from attending theatre
Beginning of building permanent
theatres in Peking

Mid 18th-late 19th century
Decline of k'un ch'u
Period of theatrical styles from
which Peking Opera developed

JAPAN AND KOREA

Yi Dynasty continues in Korea
1652 *Young men's kabuki* banned
in Japan; actors shave forelocks
Chikamatsu Monzaemon (1653-
1725), Japanese playwright
doll and *kabuki* theatre
Ichikawa Danjuro I (1660-1704),
Japanese *kabuki* actor and
playwright

1664 *The Outcast's Revenge* by
Fukui Yagozaemon in Osaka, 1st
full-length *kabuki* play

1685 Takemoto-za puppet theatre
opens in Osaka
Takemoto Gidazu (1651-1744), famous
Japanese *joruri*
1688-1720 Genroku Era of *men's kabuki*
in Japan

1715 Tachimatsu Hachirobei,
puppeteer , appears in Edo (Tokyo)
1717 1st direct *kabuki* borrowings
from Osaka puppet theatre

1725-1800 Golden Age of the Classical
Novel in Korea; many dramatized
1730's Period of popularity of
bunraku theatre in Japan
1749 *The Actor's Analects* well
known to actors in Japan
Kabuki incorporates entire puppet
repertory and surpasses puppet
theatre in popularity in Japan

World Theatre, 1650-1749

ITALY	SPAIN
1650 c. 1650 Renaissance ends	Popularity of *auto sacramental* and *comedia*
1668 *The Golden Apple*, lavish stage production by Italian designers at the Imperial Court in Vienna	
	1681 Death of Calderón signals end of the Golden Age Popularity of *comedia de magia* and *comedias heroicas*
1700 c. 1703 Ferdinando Bibiena (1657-1743) introduces angle perspective Pietro Metastasio (1698-1782), playwright Carlo Goldoni (1709-1703), playwright	1701-1713 War of Spanish Succession 1708 Caños del Perol built by Italian troupe; used for opera after 1715 1737 *Poetica* by neoclassical theorist Ignacio de Luzan (1702-1754)
1743 *The Servant of Two Masters* by Goldoni	1743 Teatro de la Cruz built 1745 Teatro del Principe built

World Theatre, 1650-1749

FRANCE

1650

Molière (Jean-Baptiste Poquelin, 1622-1673)

1658 Molière's troupe, Ilustre Théâtre, comes to Paris

1667-1677 Jean Racine (1639-1699) writes his greatest tragedies
1673 Royal Academy of Music and Dance established in Palais Royal by Jean-Baptiste Lully (1632-1687)
1680 Comédie-Française opens

1700   Alain-René LeSage (1668-1747), founder of French comic opera
Playwrights: Pierre Carlet de Chamblain de Marivaux (1668-1763), Prosper Jolyot Crébillon (1674-1762), Voltaire (Francois-Marie Arouet, 1694-1778)
1715 Death of Louis XIV
1723 Comédie Italienne made state theatre as Comédiens Ordinaries du Roi

1745-1751 Comic opera banned
1748 *The Spirit of the Laws* by Montesquieu

ENGLAND

1653-1658 The Protectorate under Oliver Cromwell
1st use of Italianate scenery in William Davenant's *The Seige of Rhodes*
1660 Davenant (1606-1668) and Thomas Killigrew (1612-1683) awarded monolopies for productions in London
1660-1700 The Restoration; Charles II (reign 1660-1685) restored to throne
1663 Drury Lane Theatre opens
1667 *Paradise Lost* by John Milton (1608-1674) published
1672 Drury Lane Theatre burns
1674 New Drury Lane opens
Playwrights: John Dryden (1611-1700), William Wycherley (1640-1716), Thomas Otway (1652-1685), William Congreve (1670-1729)

1688 The Glorious Revolution
1698 *A Short View of the Immorality and Profaneness of the English Stage* by Jeremy Collier (1631-1700)

1700 *The Way of the World* by Congreve
Playwrights: Colley Cibber (1671-1757), Mrs. Susannah Ce `ntlivre (1667-1723), Joseph Addison (1672-1719), Nicholas Rowe (1675-1718), George Farquhar (1678-1707), George Lillo (1693-1739)
1726 *Gulliver's Travels* by Jonathan Swift (1667-1745)
1728 *The Beggar's Opera* by John Gay (1685-1732)
1731 *The London Merchant* by Lillo
1737 Covent Garden opens
1737 Passage of Licensing Act
1747 David Garrick (1717-1779), actor-manager of Drury Lane

World Theatre, 1650-1749

NORTHERN AND EASTERN EUROPE	THE NEW WORLD
1650	
1650-1687 German acting troupe of Carl Andreas Pausen	
1652 Italian designers in Vienna	
1654 Italian designers in Munich	
1659 Peak of Jesuit theatre in Austria	
	1665 *Ye Bare and Ye Cubb* performed on Eastern Shore of Virginia
1672 1st record of theatre in Moscow	
In Czechoslovakia village folk comedies written by Václav Frantisek Kozmánek (1607-1679) and Karel Kolcava (1656-1717)	
1687 1st opera house in Brussels	
1690 Swedish actors established in Stockholm; classical French repertoire	1691-95 Count Frontenac produces 2 plays in Quebec
1695 György Felvinczi (c. 1650-1716), Hungarian playwright, attempts to found theatre	
1700 Hanswurst, popular German clown	
1700 Théâtre de la Monnaie in Brussels	1705 Act of Assembly of Pennsylvania against "stage-plays and revels" disallowed by England
Ludwig Holberg (1684-1754), Danish playwright	
1725-1750 Theatre in Russia largely confined to courts	1714 *Androboros* by Robert Hunter (d. 1734) earliest extant play printed in America
1727-1739 German theatre activity of Johann Gottsched (1700-1766) and Carolina Neuber (1697-1760)	1716 William Levingston builds theatre in Williamsburg
1737 Royal Swedish Theatre opens	1730's Plays performed in New York and Charles Town
1737 1st theatre built in Prague	1749 Theatre in Plumstead's Warehouse, Philadelphia
1739-1748 10 tragedies by Eric Wrangel, (1689-1765), Swedish playwright	Theatre company of Walter Murray and Thomas Kean
1744 Drottningholm Court Theatre established	

World Theatre, 1650-1749

THE MIDDLE EAST

• By mid 17th century *karagoz* was a sufficiently established form of entertainment to be trans-ported to other Middle Eastern and North African nations -- Syria, Persia, Egypt, Tunisia and Algeria.

• The French traveler, J. Chardin, published *Voyages en Perse*, three volumes, Amsterdam, 1711. As the world expanded for a growing number of travelers during the 17th and 18th centuries, the Western World learned more about Oriental countries, including their various entertainments.

INDIA AND SOUTHEAST ASIA

• *Moro-moro*, perhaps first staged in 1637, dramatized the victory of Christians over the Moors. Popular with the people as well as the governing authorities, hundreds of *moro-moro* plays were written and produced by the Spaniards, who had established rule in the Philippines in 1556-1571.

• The cultural and creative renaissance in India during the 15th and 16th centuries spurred interest in dance and folk drama. Over the next 200 years folk theatre in India expanded to include such types as *nautanki*, an operatic dance about historic heroes from Rajasthan; *ramalila* and *krishnalila*, religious pageant drama, and *swang*, secular buffoonery, from Uttar Pradesh and North India; *bhavai*, medieval tales of chivalry involving dance, music and mime, from Gujerat; *terukoothu*, street drama, from Madras; *yakshagana*, dance-drama, from Mysore; *kuchipudi*, outdoor night dance-drama, from Andhra.

• Tibetan mystery plays, representing episodes in Buddha's former existences, were played by monks in monastery enclosures in open air. They involved narrative, spectacle, song and improvised comedy.

• After the *lakon jatri* was brought to the Siamese capital, it gradually changed into a popular form called *lakon nok*, in which dance was subordinated to action in new stories involving common language and rough jokes. As time passed, *lakon nok* troupes increased in number, and plays were written by royalty. About 1750, court writers borrowed *lakon nok* techniques to create full-length dance-dramas in elegant verse called *lakon nai* (drama of women of the palace).

CHINA

• Hung Sheng (1645-1704) was a master playwright of *k'un ch'u*. Of his 11 plays, only one is extant, *The Palace of Eternal Youth*, dealing with the Emperor Ming Huang and his concubine, Yang Kuei-fei.

- Kung Shang-jen (1648-1718) wrote three plays. *The Peach Blossom Fan*, produced in 1690, dramatized the 1643-46 period when the rebel hoards that seized Peking and caused the suicide of the Emperor, were driven back by Manchu troups. In literary quality, *The Peach Blossom Fan* ranks among the greatest plays in the Chinese language.

JAPAN

- Chikamatsu Monzaemon (1653-1725), sometimes referred to as the Shakespeare of Japan, stopped writing for the *kabuki* theatre in 1685 to write approximately 100 works for the Takemoto-za (puppet theatre) in Osaka, where he made his greatest contribution to Japanese theatre, writing in the language of the day and about people from all walks of life. In general his plays are either quasi-historical or domestic in theme, such as the popular *Love Suicides at Sonezaki* (1703), *The Courier for Hell* (1711) and *Love Suicides at Amijima* (1721).

- Ichikawa Danjuro I (1660-1704), the first great *kabuki* actor, developed the masculine style of *aragoto*, best displayed in plays involving martial arts or superhuman characters. He also wrote about 150 plays.

- The Genroku Era (1688-1720, actually broadened to 1673 to 1735), marked a period of economic growth for the merchant class and a decline of power for the *samurai* class.

- After a checkered beginning, *kabuki* reached a great height of popularity during the Genroku Era. The *kabuki* stage developed from the *noh* stage, and after 1730 changed the *hashigikari* into the *hanimichi*, set at a 110-degree angle with the main stage which evolved throughout the 19th century into the huge contemporary *kabuki* stage with its elevators and turntables. The basic dramatic formula of *kabuki* is *geri-ninjo*, the conflict of obligation versus a sense of humanity. Basic role types are the *aragoto* or hero, the *onnagata* or female impersonator and the *wagato* or romantic. Performance techniques called *kata*--such as *rappo*, a vigorous style of movement, and *mei*, heightened emotions of extreme tension sometimes indicated by crossed eyes--enhance the *kabuki* theatre, as do the distinctive face painting called *kumadorir*, the intricate dance demands and the use of music. The place of *kabuki* in Japanese society and its relationship to prostitution and the gay quarters have frequently been scrutinized by government authorities.

- The doll theatre, to be known as *bunraku*, developed during the 17th century and marked its height of popularity in the mid 18th century. By the end of the century, it had nearly ceased to exist but was revived in the 19th century by Uemura Bunrakuken, who set up a theatre in Osaka and left his name to be immortalized with the art form. Highly sophisticated, *bunraku* blends the music of the *samisen* with the *joruri* singer/storyteller and the art of the puppeteers. The intricately articulated puppets, which are about 5/8 the size of an adult, are each manipulated by three puppeteers (less complicated puppets may be handled by a single puppeteer) who must be consumate actors. They perform on an elaborate stage and are assisted by black-clad stage hands, while the *joruri* narrates the story and creates the voices of all characters.

• *The Actor's Analects* is a collection of sayings, advice and admonishments from actors to actors. It includes seven pieces by different people, such as "Dust in the Ears" by Koneko Kichizaemon.

ITALY

• During the 18th century, as during the Renaissance, Italy was the source of many scenic innovations. Among the theatrical designers, the Bibiena family was extremely influential. Ferdinando's (1657-1743) designs were widely known in Bologna and Parma. Designs by other members of the family were soon recognized in the major cities of Europe. Other designers included Filippo Juvarra (1676-1736), Gaspare Mauro (c. 1657-1719) and his family, the Quaglio family (1601-1942) and the Galliari family (c. 1730-1823).

• Pietro Metastasio (1698-1782) gained a reputation as a writer of melodramas -- *Adriano in Siria* (1731) and *The Olympiad* (1733)--as well as librettos which were set to music many times.

• Carlo Goldoni (1709-1793) was Italy's greatest comic playwright, with more than 150 comedies, 83 musical dramas and ten tragedies to his credit. His objective as a playwright was to reform the *commedia dell'arte* through such plays as *The Servant of Two Masters* (1743) and *The Comic Theatre* (1750) in which he attacked the methods of the *commedia.*

SPAIN

• Spanish religious dramas, the *autos sacramentales,* continued to be popular and to be written by the same playwrights who were creating the secular drama known as *comedias.* By the second half of the 18th century, two more types of plays helped satisfy the people's love for spectacular effect -- the *comedia de magia,* in effect a magic show, and the *comedias heroicas,* a fusion of marches, scene changes and complicated plots.

• In *Poetica* (1737), Ignacio de Luzan (1702-1754) advocated neoclassical rules and condemned the linking of tragedy and comedy in a single play.

• Theatre practices changed very little in Spain during the 18th century. In Madrid the only public theatres performing Spanish drama were the Teatro de la Cruz and the Teatro del Principe. Acting troupes consisted of 16-20 performers and included women.

FRANCE

• The crowning achievement of Molière (1622-1763) was his ability to raise French comedy to the quality of French tragedy. At the Comédie-Française, "la Maison de Molière," his plays account for 1/7 of all productions between 1680 and 1920. As an actor, he abandoned the extroverted for the introverted character. In 1661 his troupe moved to the Palais-Royal and in 1665 became "The King's Players." Among his best known plays are *The Misanthrope* (1666), *The Miser* (1668) and *The Imaginary Invalid* (1673).

• The Comédie-Française was the result of the merger of Molière's troupe, which had taken over the rival troupe of the Théâtre de Marais, with the troupe of the Hôtel de Bourgogne -- hence the uniting of the three great repertories of Molière, Corneille and Racine. The Comédie-Française was obligated to preserve the heritage of French drama and to increase its repertory. Organized as a cooperative society in which each actor held a share, the Comédie-Française has enjoyed government subsidy and is now permanently at home in the Salle Richelieu.

• The acknowledged masterpiece of Jean Racine (1639-1699) is *Phèdre* (1677), in which he expressed his tragic concept within the ideals of Neoclassicism. Although Racine's career in the theatre was marked by unfortunate relationships with his contemporaries which caused him to abandon playwriting for a period, he was able to write several plays -- *Andromaque* (1667), *Berenice* (1670) and *Iphigenie* (1674) -- which established his reputation as one of the great French playwrights.

• Among the better known playwrights of the period Alain-René LeSage (1688-1747) attacked tax collectors in *Turcaret* (1709) and Marivaux (1688-1763) wrote 35 plays, such as *The Game of Love and Chance* (1730). Prosper Jolyot Crébillon (1674-1762) used the spectacle of horror in such plays as *Rhadamisthe and Zendie* (1711). Voltaire (1694-1778) wrote 53 plays, most of them tragedies, such as *Zaire* (1732). He brought Chinese drama to the West by adapting *The Orphan of China* (1755).

ENGLAND

• The Restoration (1660-1700) was marked by significant achievement in political thought, architecture (Christopher Wren) and literature (John Milton). Playwrights either followed neoclassical precepts or gave full swing to an indecorous comedy that eventually offended the moralists of society and stimulated Jeremy Collier (1631-1700) to write his *A Short View of the English Stage*. Among actors, Thomas Betterton (c. 1635-1710) was the outstanding figure on the Restoration stage.

• The most respected playwright of the Restoration was John Dryden (1611-1700), an outstanding critic in his *Essay of Dramatic Poesy* (1668) and author of some 30 plays, including his poetic tragedy of *All for Love* (1677). Thomas Otway (1652-1685), influenced by Shakespeare and the neoclassicists, wrote *Venice Preserv'd* (1682). Among the witty and elegant comic playwrights of the Restoration were William Wycherley (1640-1716), with *The Country Wife* (1675), and William Congreve (1670-1729), whose *The Way of the World* (1700) is considered the best of the period.

• During the first half of the 18th century English writers of comedy and tragedy came closer together in their new attitudes toward morality and the "sentimental." Sentimental comedy, suggesting more moral conservatism than wit and manners, found expression in the works of Colley Cibber (1671-1757), *The Careless Husband* (1704); Mrs. Susannah Centlivre (1667-1723), *The Gamester* (1705); and George Farquhar (1678-1707), *The Recruiting Officer* (1706). Diversity in the writing of tragedy during this period can be seen in *Cato* (1713) by Joseph Addison (1672-1719), *Jane Shore* (1714) by Nicholas Rowe (1675-1718) and *The London Merchant* (1731) by George Lillo (1693-1739). *Tom Thumb* (1730) by novelist Henry Fielding (1707-1754) burlesqued the tragedy of the period.

• The Licensing Act of 1737 prohibited the acting for "gain, hire or reward" of any play not previously licensed by the Lord Chamberlain and restricted authorized theatres to the City of Westminster.

NORTHERN AND EASTERN EUROPE

• German acting companies began to obtain some status through the efforts of Carl Paulsen. Johannes Velten (1640-1695), a German playwright, adapted French plays for his company which, since there were no permanent theatres, traveled constantly. By 1680 virtually all English traveling actors had left the Continent. Performances might consist of a play, serious or comic, which would have a clown figure, songs, dances and physical feats.

• By mid 17th century Italian scenic designers had visited throughout Europe. Ludovico Burnacini staged court entertainments in Vienna at the request of the Austrian emperor. Francesco Santurini opened a court theatre in Munich.

• Ludwig Holberg (1684-1754) was the first Danish playwright to write plays in the vernacular. Between 1722 and 1727 he wrote 26 plays, mainly robust medieval farces.

• In 1727 Johann Gottsched (1700-1766), an intellectual who wanted to raise the quality of German theatre, teamed up with Carolina Neuber (1697-1760) and her husband Johann, who owned a theatre troupe. Gottsched wrote *The Dying Cato* (1731), which the troupe performed regularly.

THE NEW WORLD

• Actors came to America, frequently via Jamaica, in reaction to the late Restoration adverse attitude toward actors in England. Traveling actors played scattered performances in Williamsburg, Charles Town, Philadelphia and New York City, sometimes being forced to circumvent existing laws against stage plays. The first serious attempt to bring theatre to America was made by Murray and Kean in 1749. There were, however, also scattered groups of colonists who contrived to act, such as the one that performed *Ye Bare and Ye Cubb* in Virginia. The two plays known during the 1650-1749 period --*Ye Bare and Ye Cubb* and *Androboros* -- suggest the form of drama that would persist in America: satiric comedy.

World Theatre, 1750-1849

THE MIDDLE EAST AND AFRICA

1750 Ottoman Empire continues
c. 1750 Processions and narrations
give birth to *Ta'zieh*
c. 1750 Popular theatre forms in Iran:
*hachalak bazi, baqqal bazi,
ruband bazi*

c. 1790 Rise of popular Turkish
theatre, *orta oyunu*
1798-1801 French occupation ends
Turkish domination of Egypt
1800

1823 1st report of the *ruhozi*, a
form of Persian comedy
1828 Turkish Sultan Mahmuh II invites
Guiseppe Donizetti, Italian,
to start orchestra and band
c. 1830's Africa open to exploration
1839 500-seat theatre built in Istanbul
Political importance of *meddahs* grows
Marun Naqqash (1817-1855), Lebanese
playwright
1848 1st play in Arabic performed
in Beirut
1849 Developing Western influence on
Ottoman Empire

INDIA AND SOUTHEAST ASIA

1756 British theatre in Calcutta
1767 Court drama introduced to
Burma by Siamese courtiers
1767 Ayudhia Period ends in Siam
1770 British theatre in Bombay

1782-1809 Rama I (Siam) has
court poets compose versions of
Panji stories for *lakon nai*
1795 1st translation of English play
into Bengali: *Disguise*

1809-1824 Rama II (Siam) composes
complete Panji story for *lakon nai*
1816 Indian *Asiatic Journal* essay
mentions *jatras* (folk theatre)
1820 Viet Nam Emperor Gia Long
builds palace theatre for *hat boy*
Burma creates Ministry of Theatre
Wealthy Calcutta citizens stage
private *jatra*
c. 1830 *Ludruk lerog,* Indonesian
entertainment

c. 1849 *Zarzuela,* from Spain,
performed in Philippines

World Theatre, 1750-1849

CHINA

1750 Ching Dynasty continues;
many theatres built
Wei Ch'ang-sheng (1744-1802),
actor

1777 Emperor Ch'ien-lung (reign 1736-
1796) creates commission to revive
theatre

1790 Theatre companies celebrating
Emperor's 80th birthday introduce
basic elements of Peking Opera
1799 Theatre banned by Emperor
1800 Decline of *k'un ch'u* begins
1802 Theatre banned by Emperor

Ch'eng Chang-keng (1812-1880),
Father of Peking Opera
c. 1830 Beginnings of Peking Opera
1839-1842 Opium War

JAPAN AND KOREA

Yi Dynasty continues in Korea
c. 1750 *P'ansori* has fixed repertory
of 12 stories in Korea

Sande togam, entertainment
officials in Korea, cease to exist
Sin Chae-hyo (1812-1884), teacher
and arranger of Korean *p'ansori*
Japanese songs and dances broaden
themes to include life of common
people
Kizewamono ("raw" or domestic
play) depicts seamy side of life
in Japan

1840 *The Subscription List* by
Namiki Gohei III (1790-1855),
Japanese playwright

World Theatre, 1750-1849

ITALY

1750 *The Comic Theatre* by Goldoni
Carlo Gozzi (1720-1806) attempts to
to reform *commedia* with new
form, *fiabe*
Gian Battista Piranesi (1720-1778),
designer
Vittorio Alfieri (1749-1803),
playwright
1762-1773 Goldoni in Paris writing
for *comedie italienne*

1800 French Revolutionary Wars
affect Italian theatre
Lorenzo Sacchetti (1759-1829),
designer
Alessandro Sanquirico (1777-1849),
designer for Teatro alla Scala
in Milan
1814-1815 Congress of Vienna
1816 Naples and Sicily united
Giambattista Niccolini (1782-
1861), romantic playwright
Alessandro Manzoni (1785-
1873), romantic playwright

SPAIN

1765 Prohibition of *autos
sacramentales* by neo-classicists

1773 Official support for tragedies
declines
1778 *Racquel* by Vicente Farcia de
la Huerta (1734-1787) shows
neoclassical principles
Sainetes, short farces reflecting
everyday life in Madrid
Ramón de la Cruz (1731-1794),
writer of *sainete*

1806 *When a Girl Says Yes*, neoclassical comedy, by Leandro
Fernández de Moratín (1760-1828)
1808 Napoleon's brother crowned
king

1814-1833 Repressive government
under Ferdinand VII

1834 *The Venice Conspiracy*, 1st
quasi romantic play, by Francisco
Martinez de la Rosa (1787-1862)
Late 1840's Decline of romantic
drama
1849 Theatre reform begins

World Theatre, 1750-1849

FRANCE

1750 1748-1772 Denis Diderot (1713-1784) edits *Encyclopedie*
1751 Revival of *opera comique*
Beaumarchais (Pierre-Augustin Caron, 1732-1799), playwright
c. 1759 Spectators banned from stage
c. 1760 Boulevard theatre begins
1769-1780 Popularity of *opera comique* and plays of Goldoni

1789-1815 French Revolution
1791 National Assembly abolishes theatre monolopies
1793 Louis XVI guillotined
1800 c. 1800 François-Joseph Talma (1763-1826), actor
1806-1831 Napoleon's restrictive acts affect theatre
1810 Guilbert de Pixérécourt (1773-1844), playwright; melodrama flourishes
1815 Battle of Waterloo
Eugene Scribe (1791-1861), author of well-made plays
1827 *Preface to Cromwell* by Victor Hugo (1802-1885)
1828 Publication of *Livrets Sceneques*
1830 *Hernani* by Hugo marks beginning of Romanticism
1839 Invention of photography
1840's Increased emphasis on Realism in scene, illumination and costume
Playwrights: Alfred de Vigny (1797--1863), Alexandre Dumas, *père* (1802-1870), Alfred de Musset (1810-1857)

ENGLAND

c. 1750 Styles of acting change from oratorical to natural
1752 Licensing Bill for theatres 20 miles outside London

1762 David Garrick (1717-1779), actor-manager, bans audience from stage
1766 Haymarket Theatre opens
1771-1785 Design contributions of Philippe Jacques de Loutherbourg (1740-1812)
Playwrights: Hugh Kelly (1739-1777), Richard Cumberland (1732-(1732-1811), Thomas Holcroft (1745-1809), Oliver Goldsmith (1730?-1774), Richard Brinsley Sheridan (1751-1816)
1785 Introduction of Argand lamp
1792-1794 Patent theatres enlarged

1800-1817 John Philip Kemble (1757-1823), manager of Covent Garden
1800-1836 Period of classical acting style of Kemble family
Playwrights: James Sheridan Knowles (1784-1862), Douglas Jerrold (1803-1857), Edward Bulwer-Lytton (1803-1873)
1823 Historically accurate costumes in *King John,* acted by Charles Kemble (1775-1854)
William Macready (1793-1873), actor-manager
1833 Royal Victoria ("Old Vic")
Madame Vestris (1797-1856), manager of Olympic Theatre (1831-1839)
1843 Theatre Regulation Act abolishes patent theatres' privileges
1848 Karl Marx's *The Communist Manifesto*

GERMANY

1750   Gotthold Ephraim Lessing (1729-1781), playwright

1756-1763 Seven Years War
1767 Hamburg National Theatre opens
1767-1769 Lessing's *Hamburg Dramaturgy*
1767-1787 *Sturm und Drang* movement
1770-1800 Influential troupe of Friedrich Ludwig Schröder (1744-1816)
1773 *Göetz von Berlichingen* by Johann Wolfgang von Goethe (1749-1832)
1776 Emperor Joseph II founds Imperial and National Theatre (Burgtheater)
1780 State theatres established in German-speaking areas
1782 *The Robbers* by Friedrich Schiller (1759-1805)
1792 Goethe placed in control of Weimar Court Theatre

1800

1805-c. 1825 Theatre restricted during French occupation and Metternich Regine

Major playwrights: August von Kotzebue (1761-1819), Heinrich von Kleist (1777-1811), Georg Büchner (1813-1837), Friedrich Hebbel (1813-1863)

1830-1848 Young Germany movement

NORTHERN EUROPE

Swedish King Gustav III (1746-1792), actor and playwright
1750-1850 Swedish theatre companies tour Finland

John Herman Wessel (1742-1785), Norwegian playwright
1770 1st amateur dramatic society in Christiana (Oslo)
1773 Royal Theatre of Copenhagen opens
1774 New Amsterdam Theatre opens
1775-1800 Swedish drama submissive to French Neoclassicism

1788 Royal Swedish Dramatic Theatre founded

1793 Arsenal Theatre opens in Stockholm
1800-c. 1840's Swedish theatre continues decline

1812-1827 Carl Gustaf Bonuvier 1776-1858), Finnish theatre entrepreneur
Dutch drama influenced by French Neoclassicism

1827 1st attempt to start theatre in Norway
Dutch playwrights: Johan Ludwig (1791-1860), Henrik Hertz (1798-1870)

Revolutions of 1848

RUSSIA

LATIN AMERICA

1750

1752 1st theatre company in Russia

Alexander Sumarokov (1717-1777),
  playwright
1756 State theatre established in
  St. Petersburg
Denis Fonvizin (1745-1792),
  playwright

1786-1823 Regulations of Viceroy
  stifle theatre in Mexico

1790 2nd state theatre opens in
  St. Petersburg
1790-1810 Serf theatres popular

1793 1st theatre in Bogota

1800 19th century Russian theatre
  expands throughout century
1805 State theatre opens in Moscow;
  training school established
Playwrights: Vladislav Ozerov (1770-
  1816), Alexander Griboyedov (1795-
  1829), Alexander Pushkin (1799-
  1837), Mikhail Lermontov (1814-
  1841), Nikolai Gogol (1809-1852)
Mikhail Shchepin (1781-1863), 1st
  great Russian-born actor

1820 1st permanent theatre in Chile
  opens with Addison's *Cato*
Luis Vargas Tayada (1802-1829),
  Colombia's 1st national play-
  wright
1837 1st permanent theatre in San José
Playwrights: Fernando Calderón
  (1809-1845, Mexico), Francisco
  Xavier de Acha (1828-1888,
  Paraguay), José Fernandez
  Madrid (1780-1830, Colombia),
  Carlos Bello (1815-1854, Chile),
  José Joaquin de Olmedo (1780-
  1847, Equador)

World Theatre, 1750-1849

COLONIAL AMERICA/THE UNITED STATES

1750

1752-1754 Lewis Hallam (1714-1756) and his Company of Comedians

1758 David Douglass (?-1786), manager, American Company of Comedians

1767 *The Prince of Parthia* by Thomas Godfrey (1736-1763)

1773-1776 Revolutionary drama; Mercy Warren (1728-1814), playwright

1774 Continental Congress forbids all "shows and plays"

1776-1783 War of Independence

1787 *The Contrast* by Royall Tyler (1757-1826)

William Dunlap (1766-1839), playwright, historian, manager

1798-1848 Park Theatre in New York

1800 John Howard Payne (1791-1852), actor-playwright

1815 Westward movement of theatre begins

Edwin Forrest (1806-1872), actor

1828 1st of Forrest's 9 playwriting contests

1829 1st contest winner *Metamora,* by John Augustus Stone (1801-1834)

Robert Montgomery Bird (1806-1854), playwright

George Handel Hill (1809-1849), Yankee actor

Thomas D. Rice (1808-1860), "Jim Crow" imitator

1839-1850 Olympic Theatre in New York

1843 Virginia Minstrels

The Drunkard by William S. Smith (1806-1872)

1845 *Fashion* by Anna Cora Mowatt Ritchie (1819-1870)

1846 *Witchcraft* by Cornelius Mathews (1817-1889), Father of American Drama

1848 *A Glance at New York* by Benjamin A. Baker (1818-1890)

1849 Astor Place Riot

World Theatre, 1750-1849

THE MIDDLE EAST AND AFRICA

• The *Ta'zieh*, the Shi'ite mourning ritual, is Islam's only indigenous drama. The organic development of the *Ta'zieh* during the late 18th century makes it difficult to determine the authorship of any particular written text, which is essentially only a guide for performance. By the 19th century the *Ta'zieh* was performed as a complete dramatic form which encompassed a cycle of plays, such as "The Martyrdom of Ali-Akabar, Son of Hussain" or "The Martyrdom of Iman Hussain," many now existing in different versions. All commemorate an historical event and become a parable of suffering in the battle of good and evil. The historical procession and recitation of the poetic texts become the raw material for the religious and theatrical passion play. Acting conventions, dance, music, performance styles and color-coded costumes to designate antagonists and protagonists suggest the appeal of the *Ta'zieh* to both ear and eye.

• During the H*achalak bazi* ("play of the bald") denounced the rich, the dishonest and the depraved. The *baqqal bazi* ("the play of the grocer") were built around a miserly grocer and his stupid servant. Both forms lacked texts and were similar to the *commedia dell'arte*. The *ruband bazi* ("the play of the mask") features actors on stilts.

• The origins of *orta oyunu*, the Turkish version of *commedia dell'arte*, are impossible to determine. As a play "in the middle" (*orta* meaning "middle" and *oyunu* meaning "play or spectacle"), it features *taklid* or mimicry and has existed at least since the 18th century. Usually it is performed in an outdoor oval area about 30 yards by 20 yards with few properties (a chair and a winged screen) and music off stage. The chief players are Pishekiar, a clever conjurer who rarely leaves the stage and dresses in a yellow gown, red tunic and a cap of many colors, and Kavuklu, a comic trader or servant who wears a red gown and has an enormous hat. Zenne is the female (always played by men), and lesser characters include a rake, a Persian, an Arab, a drunkard, a Jew, and a Georgian. These plays begin with a parade of the characters and have two parts: a quarrel between Pishekiar and Kavuklu, interrupted by Zenne, and a skit involving disguises, exaggerations, language confusion and all kinds of horseplay. Comparisons with the *karagoz* are clear.

• The Persian comedy called *ruhozi* ("over the pool") was so named because the stage was erected over a tank, usually in an open courtyard. Principal characters include Siyah ("the black"), who blackened his face and spoke with an accent to suggest a former slave, and Haji, a rich man.

• The beginnings of Arab modern drama occurred in 1848 with the production in Beirut of *The Miser* (inspired by Molière's work but not imitative of it) at the home of the author, Marun Naqqash (1817-1850). Called the Father of Arabic Theatre, Naqqash traveled in Syria, Egypt and Italy before writing his plays, which incorporate prose, poetry, singing and musical instruments in the manner of European opera.

• Kings of Siam were serious patrons of theatre as composers -- particularly King Rama II (of *The King and I* fame) -- and as observers of *lakon nai, khon* and *nang yai*.

• The Indian *Asiatic Journal* (1816) noted that "*jatras* of this season were chiefly dramatic representations of the loves of Krishna and the milk maids."

• Burma was the first country in the world to create a Ministry of Theatre. Its traditional theatre is called *pwe* (something "shown"), of which a number of types exist: *zat pwe*, classical dance-dramas on the life of Buddha; *yokthe pwe*, puppet theatre; *nat pwe*, an ancient spirit dance.

• The *ludruk lerog*, from Java, was an improvised folk dance featuring two men: a clown and a female impersonator.

• *Zarzuela*, of uncertain beginnings in the Philippines, was a light opera with anti-colonial themes.

CHINA

• In contrast to earlier limited interest in court and temple theatre, emperors during the Ching Dynasty (1644-1911), particularly Ch'ien-lung (reign 1736-1796), built a large number of theatres. Basically, these theatres were of four types for different occasions: a place for celebrations such as birthdays or weddings, a less formal restaurant theatre, a small theatre open to everyone and the popular *hsi-yüan*, the very informal and noisy social institution -- "like ten thousand crows cawing in competition" -- which opened at dawn and closed at sunset. Watching continuous entertainment, *hsi-yüan* audience members chanted, drank tea or bargained with the innumerable peddlers.

• As *k'un ch'u* began to decline in popularity, other opera styles appeared. The four styles from which Peking Opera eventually emerged were *yi-yang ch'iang, pang-tzu* or clapper opera, *hsi-p'i* and *erh-huang*, which was solemn and lyrical. Performers of the last two styles came from Anhwei to Peking for the Emperor's birthday celebration in 1790. Wei Ch'ang-sheng (1744-1802), one of the greatest actors of the clapper style, had come to Peking in 1782. From these basic musical and performance elements assembled in 1790 Peking Opera gained its identity.

• The primary actor in *k'un ch'u* had been the *tan* or female impersonator. With the beginnings of Peking Opera and the change from civil to military dramas (and the stronger musical interpretation changing from flute and string to percussion), the most popular actors now performed the *sheng* (hero) or *lao-sheng* (old men) roles. The first of the great *lao-sheng* actors was Ch'eng Chang-keng (1812-1880).

JAPAN AND KOREA

• The *p'ansori* was a solo performance established in the 17th and 18th centuries. By the middle of the 18th century performers had collected twelve stories for their repertory, all of which were transmitted orally. Sin Chae-hyo (1812-1884) rearranged the twelve pieces into six, which he transcribed into a written text.

• After 1800 the officials (*sandae togam*), traditionally appointed throughout the Yi Dyansty (1392-1910), ceased to be appointed, with the result that plays came under the control of professional actors.

• *The Subscription List* (1840) by Namiki Gohei III (1790-1855), a *kabuki* masterpiece written and performed in the manner of the *noh*, is particularly important because it served, with certain other plays, to fuse two major theatrical art forms of Japan. In general, *noh* actors had previously regarded *kabuki* actors as social and artistic outcasts, which, at various points in history, had been true.

ITALY

• The *fiabe* was a mixture of fantasy and fooling. Examples of attempts by Carlo Gozzi (1720-1800) include *The Love of Three Oranges* (1761) and *Turandot* (1762).

• Continuing their dominance in theatrical design throughout Europe, such designers as Piranesi (1720-1778) became influential for their use of light and shadow to create mood. Paolo Landriani (1770-1838) employed the box set in the late 18th century, although he may not have been the first to do so.

• The upheaval caused by Napoleon affected the writing of drama during the first half of the 19th century, as well as Italian influence in both theatrical design and the opera. Dramatic writing depreciated; theatre companies were forced to tour in order to survive.

SPAIN

• At the middle of the 18th century the traditionalists from the Golden Age in Spain, though few in number, were attempting to support the theories of Ignacio de Luzan's (1702-1754) *Poetica* (1737). They were able to prohibit the *autos sacramentales* but not the *comedias de magia*. *Racquel* (1773) was a minor neoclassical success, but far more popular were the *sainetes*, short sketches in verse.

• If neoclassical tragedy waned, neoclassical comedy found a master in the work of Leandro Fernández de Moratín (1760-1828). Soon, however, the armies of Napoleon, followed by the autocracy of Ferdinand VII, caused artists and writers to leave Spain for

France, England and Germany. There they learned of the new Romanticism, which became popular in Spain from the mid 1830's to the mid 1840's.

FRANCE

• Denis Diderot (1713-1784) foreshadowed Realism in his concern for *le drame* and promoted a reevaluation of traditional concepts in the *Encyclopedie*. Only Beaumarchais (1732-1799) during this period added substantially to French drama with such plays as *The Barber of Seville* (1775) and *The Marriage of Figaro* (1783).

• About 1760 the Boulevard du Temple became a fashionable spot for the activities of such companies as Audinot's, Nicolet's, the Théâtre des Associés and the Varietiés Amusantes.

• Guilbert de Pixérécourt (1773-1844), the master of early 19th century melodrama, employed spectacle, sentimentality, emotionalism, bourgeois morality and a degree of sensationalism. His best melodrama was *Victor; or, The Child of the Forest* (1798).

• Eugene Scribe (1791-1861), the author of more than 300 plays, is best known as the originator of the well-made play, a play that is carefully constructed with well motivated characters and a clear plot in which all actions are carefully resolved and explained. An illustration of Scribe's work is *A Glass of Water* (1840).

ENGLAND

• Government regulations for theatres became more widespread and complicated as theatres throughout the British Isles were once again legal. David Garrick (1717-1779) continued his influential work under a wide range of banners -- importing de Loutherbourg from Paris, making innovations in lighting, playwriting, acting, theatre management and the training of actors.

• Domestic tragedy declined as sentimental comedy began to flourish with the works of Hugh Kelly (1739-1777), *False Delicacy* (1768); Richard Cumberland (1732-1811), *The West Indian* (1771); Thomas Holcroft (1745-1809), *The Road to Ruin* (1792). Reacting to this form of comedy, Oliver Goldsmith (1730?-1774) wrote *She Stoops to Conquer* (1773), and Richard Brinsley Sheridan (1751-1816) contributed *The Rivals* (1775) and *The School for Scandal* (1779).

• With the beginning of the 19th century, English actors and managers gained ascendance as playwrights languished. Notable poets and novelists tried to write plays and in general failed to please the public: Samuel Taylor Coleridge (1772-1834), William Wordsworth (1770-1850), John Keats (1795-1821), Percy Bysshe Shelley (1792-1822), Lord Byron (1788-1824), Sir Walter Scott (1771-1832) and Robert Browning (1812-1889). Browning had minor success with *A Blot on the 'Scutcheon* (1843); all of Byron's plays were produced; Shelley's *The Cenci* (1819) and *Prometheus Unbound* (1820) were not staged during his lifetime.

• The popular playwrights of the day have not survived the test of time: Joanna Baillie (1762-1851), *De Montfort* (1800); Sheridan Knowles (1784-1862), *Virginius* (1820); Douglas Jerrold (1803-1857), *Black-Eyed Susan* (1829); John B. Buckstone (1802-1879), *Luke the Labourer* (1826); and Edward Bulwer-Lytton (1803-1873) *The Lady of Lyons* (1838).

• Among actors, the Kemble family -- from John Philip Kemble (1757-1823) and his sister Sarah Kemble Siddons (1755-1831), to Eliza Kemble Whitlock (1761-1836), Charles Kemble (1775-1854) and his daughter Fanny Kemble (1809-1893) -- dominated the stage. Providing a romantic challenge to their stately classical style were George Frederich Cooke (1756-1812) and Edmund Kean (1787-1833). William Macready (1793-1873) excelled as both actor and manager but is remembered in America largely for his role in the Astor Place Riot of 1849. Madame Vestris (1797-1856) was a successful manager of the Olympic Theatre in London, assisted by J. R. Planché (1795-1880), a prolific writer of burlesques and extravaganzas.

GERMANY

• German theatre during the last half of the 18th century is dominated by the work of Gotthold Lessing (1729-1781), whose *Miss Sara Sampson* (1755) was Germany's most popular middle-class domestic tragedy, and his *Minna von Barnhelm* (1867) Germany's first national comedy. Through his *Hamburg Dramaturgy* (1767-1769), he argued against Johann Gottsched's (1700-1766) interest in French neoclassical writers and insisted upon English plays as appropriate models for the German stage.

• The *Sturm und Drang* ("Storm and Stress") movement was a somewhat disorganized and certainly diverse revolt against Neoclassicism and 18th century Rationalism.

• Johann Wolfgang von Goethe (1749-1832) and Friedrich Schiller (1759-1805), Germany's substantial playwrights of the period, provided more lasting exceptions within a mass of unremarkable plays. Eventually working together, they improved upon the popular illusionary drama of their contemporaries to create a tranformation of ordinary life to universal understanding. Their ideas became known as Weimar Classicism.

• The most popular playwrights of the late 18th century were August Wilhelm Iffland (1759-1814) and August Friederich von Kotzebue (1761-1819). Kotzebue, the author of more than 200 melodramas, had the greater international appeal with such plays as *Menschenhaus und Reue* (1789).

• The political difficulties of the early decades of the 19th century had a stultifying effect upon the theatre. Of the romanticists, only August Wilmelm Schlegel (1767-1845) and Ludwig Tieck (1773-1853) contributed substantially with both plays and essays. Among playwrights, the best -- Heinrich von Kleist (1777-1811) with *The Broken Jug* (1806) and Georg Büchner (1813-1837) with *Danton's Death* (1835) and *Woyzeck* (1836) -- were largely ignored. Friederich Hebbel (1813-1863) was drawn to G. W. F. Hegel's philosophy and with *Maria Magdalena* (1844) brought some distinction to a German theatre, which seriously declined after his death.

• Among German actors were Ludwig Devrient (1784-1832), Ferdinand Esslain (1772-1840) and Bogumil Dawison (1818-1872). Johann Nestroy (1801-1862), Austrian actor and playwright, contributed 83 plays to Austrian folk drama.

NORTHERN EUROPE

• The Swedish theatre was fortunate to have an indulgent king, Gustav III, who encouraged a slowly developing theatre during the last half of the 18th century. When he died, the Swedish theatre declined, and Swedish actors traveled to other countries.

• French Neoclassicism was a strong influence in Sweden and in the Netherlands. Shakespeare was emphasized in the Royal Theatre of Copenhagen after 1773, along with German domestic drama, which the Dutch also appreciated. Johan Ludwig (1791-1860) introduced French vaudeville to Denmark.

RUSSIA

• The first theatre company in Russia was established by Fyodor Volkov (c. 1729-1763). Much theatrical activity centered in St. Petersburg, but touring theatre companies played other major cities, and wealthy land owners began to select and train performers in what were called "serf theatres." In Moscow in 1797, there were 17 serf theatres.

• Although by 1750 the Russian court was aware of Western theatre, there was no public theatre in Russia and no native repertory. The first playwright of distinction, Alexander Sumarokov (1717-1777), wrote on Russian subjects but used the French neoclassical form. Denis Fonvizin (1745-1792) also used Russian material in such comedies as *The Brigadier General* (1766).

• Political problems relative to the Napoleonic era and the repressions that followed in Russia affected the theatre. *Woe and Wit* (1822-1825) by Alexander Griboyedov (1795-1829) is the single important Russian play in neoclassical style, but censorship kept it out of the theatre. *Boris Gudonov* (1825) by Alexander Pushkin (1799-1837) was kept off the stage until 1870. *Masquerade* (1835) by Mikhail Lermontov (1814-1841) was denied production. Nikolai Gogol's (1809-1852) *The Inspector General* (1836), was produced but also viciously attacked.

• Throughout Russian theatre of this period scenic practices were not innovative, although Prince Alexander Shakhovskoz (1777-1847), Director of Repertory in the Imperial Theatre (1801-1826) promoted expansions and new rules for state theatres.

LATIN AMERICA

• Prior to 1850 the countries of Latin America had few theatres and produced no distinctive drama. With repressive governments using drama for propaganda, the church trying to prohibit theatre and critics crying for "native plays about Indians and local color," playwrights faced a difficult task. Argentina, Mexico, Paraguay, Peru and Venezuela endured amateur attempts at theatre or had nothing at all.

COLONIAL AMERICA/THE UNITED STATES

• Called the Father of American Theatre, William Dunlap (1766-1839) managed the Park Theatre in New York and saved more than one season by writing plays -- *André* (1798) among them -- and adapting works from the French and the German.

• As the theatre began to move westward after the War of 1812, touring circuits were established that would eventually include such cities as Mobile, St. Louis and New Orleans. Noah Ludlow (1795-1886) and Sol Smith (1801-1869) were eager entrepreneurs in this theatre expansion.

• America's first great native-born actor was Edwin Forrest (1806-1872), who established playwriting contests from which he purchased some of his best acting roles: *Metamora; or, The Last of the Wampanoags* (1829), his first winning play, by John Augustus Stone (1801-1834) and *The Gladiator* (1831) and *The Broker of Bogota* (1834) by Robert M. Bird (1806-1854), whose disappointment in Forrest's treatment caused him to stop writing plays. Forrest's ego precipitated a feud with English actor William Macready that caused a partisan crowd to riot on May 10, 1849 in the Astor Place Opera House. Thirty-one people were killed when police fired into the mob.

• During the 1840's the Olympic Theatre of William Mitchell (1798-1856) was the only theatre in New York making money -- largely because it produced parodies such as *Metamora; or, The Last of the Polywogs* (1847) by John Brougham (1810-1880) and spectacles such as *A Glance at New York* (1848) by Benjamin A. Baker (1818-1890). Frank Chanfrau (1824-1884) made his reputation playing Mose the Bowery B'hoy in *A Glance at New York* and the various spin-offs that followed.

World Theatre, 1850-1915

THE MIDDLE EAST AND AFRICA

1850 1850-1855 Mirza Fathali
Akhundzadeh (1812-1878), Persian
comic writer
1853-1856 David Livingston in Africa

1859 Modern drama begins in Turkey
1860 Gedikpasa Theatre built in Turkey
1860 *The Poet's Marriage,* 1st Turkish
play, by Ibrahim Sinasi (1826-1871)

1869 Cairo Opera House completed
1870-1884 Ottoman Theatre Company
holds monolopy of Turkish theatre;
Gullu Agop (1840-1902), manager

1875 1876 Brussels conference for
"civilizing stations" in Africa
Uthman Jalal (1829-1898), Egyptian
playwright
Turkish playwrights: Namik Kemal
(1840-1888), Ali Bey (1844-1899),
Ahmet Efendi (1844-1912), Abdulah
Hamid (1852-1937)
Late 19th century Mirza Âqâ Tabrizi,
1st Persian playwright
Jacob Sanou (1839-1912), the "Molière
of Egypt"
Abou Khaili al Kabbani (1836-1902),
founder of 1st theatre in Damascus
1899-1902 Boer War
Late 19th century-1908 Hamidian
rule censorship in Turkey
1900
1905 Lovers of the Hebrew Stage in Jaffa
Jurj Abyad (1880-1962), Lebanese
producer, hired by Khedive of Egypt
1911 National Theatre founded in Iran
1914 Municipal Theatre and School of
Dance and Music open in Istanbul

INDIA

Mid-19th century Marathi theatre
known for boisterous comedies:
Vishnudas Bhave's *The Marriage
of Sita*

1857 Sepoy Indian Mutiny

1864 *The Tragic Plight of Lalila,* by
R. Bhoi Udayram, Gujarati
1865 Kekhushru Kabraji, 1st Gujarati
playwright, founds theatre
1870 Parsi businessmen in Bombay
found 1st professional company to
use Hindi language
1872 Girish Chandra Ghosh (1814-
1911), founds National Theatre and
1st Bengali professional troupe
1876 Dramatic Performance Act
1877 Queen Victoria proclaimed
Empress of India
Bharatendu Harishchander (1850-
1885), Father of Hindi Drama
D. Krishnamachari, Father of
Telugu-Language Theatre
G. Appa Rao (1861-1915), author of 1st
important social-realistic play in
Telugu, *The Sale of a Virgin Girl*
D. L. Roy (1863-1913), Bengali
author of farces and historical
plays; *Shah Jahan* (1909)

1913 Rabindranath Tagore (1861-
1941), Bengali, wins Nobel Prize
1914 British start theatre in Punjab

World Theatre, 1850-1915

SOUTHEAST ASIA

1850 Traditional theatre forms
continue

1870-1942 Dutch Empire rules
Indonesia
1870 *Bangsawan* starts in Penang

1875 *Makyong* dance-drama in
Malaysia

1898 United States annexes Philippines
1900 Burmese *zat pwe*, stories of Buddha
Burmese *yim pwe*, religious dance-drama
Balinese *rangda-barong*, dance-drama
Malaysian *manohra*, dance-drama
Indonesian *ludruk besut*, clown drama
1910-1925 Rama VI (Siam) writes drama
1911 Siamese theatrical forms: *liki*,
hun, nang, lakon, khon, manora

CHINA

1850-1864 Taiping Rebellion

1870-1900 Golden Age of Peking
Opera

1889 Missionary colleges in
Shanghai foster interest in
Western drama

1900 Boxer Rebellion
1902 Amateur Western performances
at St. John University in Shanghai
1907 *Uncle Tom'a Cabin* performed
in Shanghai
1911 Revolution, Ching Dynasty falls
Wen-ming-hsi (the civilized play)
1911-1912 Association of New
Dramatists

World Theatre, 1850-1915

JAPAN AND KOREA

1850 Yi Dynasty continues in Korea
Korean musical drama begins;
Sin Che-Ho (1812-1884)

1867 Tokugawa Period ends in
Japan
1868 Meiji Era begins in Japan

1875

1881 Modern Liberal Theatre
movement in Japan
1880's New School Theatre
(*shimpa*) under Kawakami
Otojiro (1864-1911) in Japan
1888 *Soshi geki*, political drama
in Japan
Kawatake Mokuami (1816-1893),
last great writer of *kabuki*
Kabuki actors: Danjuro IX (1838-
1903) and Sadanji I (1842-1904)
1890's *Shinsei shimpa*, or New Life
New School begins in Japan
1900 1905 Japan annexes Korea
1908 1st National Korean Theatre, Seoul
Yi In-Jig (1861-1916), Korean playwright
c. 1909 *Shingeki* (new theatre) in Japan
imports Western theatre
1910-1945 Japan rules Korea
1911 Neo-*kabuki* play, *Tale of Shugenji*
by Okamoto Kido (1872-1939)
1911-1920 Drama Reform Society in Korea

ITALY AND SPAIN

1861 Unification of Italy under
Victor Emmanuel

1867 *A New Drama* by Spanish play-
wright Tamayo y Baus (1829-1898)
Popularity of *alta comedia* in
Spain

1875 José Echegaray (1832-1916),
Spanish playwright
Paolo Ferrari (1822-1889), Italian
playwright of realistic school

1898 "Generation of 1898" group
dissatisfied with Spanish drama
1898 Teatro Intim founded in Barcelona
by Adria Gual (1872-1932)
Jacinto Benavente (1866-1954), Spanish
playwright
Italian actors: Tommaso Salvini (1829-
1915), Eleanora Duse (1859-1924)
Gabriele d'Annunzio (1863-1938),
Italian playwright
1913 *The Tragic Sense of Life* by Miguel
de Unamuno (1864-1936), Spain

World Theatre, 1850-1915

FRANCE

1850
1851 *The Italian Straw Hat* by
  Eugene Labiche (1815-1888)
1852 *Camile* by Alexandre Dumas
  fils (1824-1895)
1860 *A Scrap of Paper* by Victorien
  Sardou (1831-1908)
1860's Boulevard du Temples disappears
François Delsarte (1811-1871) originates
  system of stage expressions

1874 Paris Opera completed
1875 Adolphe Montigne (1805-1880), director
1881 *Naturalism in the Theatre* by
  Emile Zola (1849-1902)
1882 *The Vultures,* naturalistic play,
  by Henri Becque (1837-1899)
1887 Théâtre Libre founded
1890-1892 Théâtre d'Art, symbolist interest
Actors: Constantine Benoît Coquelin (1841-
  1909), Sarah Bernhardt (1849-1923)
1892-1899 Théâtre de l'Oeuve founded
Adolph Appia (1862-1928); *The Staging
  of Wagner's Musical Dramas* (1895),
  Music and Stage Setting (1899)
1896 *Ubu Roi* by Alfred Jarry (1873-1907)
1897 Théâtre Antoine opens
1900 Freud's *Interpretation of Dreams*
Eugene Brieux (1858-1932), playwright

Paul Claudel (1869-1955), playwright

1913-1914 Théâtre de Vieux Colombier
  of Jacques Copeau (1879-1949)

ENGLAND AND IRELAND

1850-1870 Popularity of English
  burlesque-extravaganza
1859 *The Origin of Species* by Charles
  Darwin (1809-1892)
1860-1880 Bancrofts manage Prince of
  Wales Theatre
Thomas W. Robertson (1829-1872),
  playwright
1871-1896 Comic operas of W. S. Gilbert
  (1836-1911) and Arthur Sullivan
  (1842-1900)

1880-1900 Dominance of Henry Irving
  (1838-1905), actor-manager
1886 International Copyright Agreement
Playwrights: Henry Arthur Jones
  (1851-1929), Arthur Wing Pinero
  (1855-1934), George Bernard Shaw
  (1856-1950), Oscar Wilde (1856-1900)
1891-1897 Independent Theatre; J.T.
  Grein (1862-1935), manager
1894 Elizabethan Stage Society;
  William Poel (1852-1934), head

Herbert Beerbohm Tree (1853-1917),
  actor-manager
1899 Irish dramatic movement
1904-1907 Court Theatre Company
1904 Abbey Theatre opens in Dublin
Playwrights: James M. Barrie (1861-
  1937), John Galsworthy (1867-1933)
1905 *The Art of the Theatre* by Gordon
  Craig (1862-1966)
1910 Irish National Theatre Society
John Millington Synge (1871-1909),
  Irish playwright

World Theatre, 1850-1915

GERMANY AND CENTRAL EUROPE

1850 State support for German theatres

1853-1887 Professional Flemish theatre
   in Belgium
Imre Madách (1823-1864), Hungarian
   playwright; *The Tragedy of Man*
   (1860)

Kendrik Jan Schimmel (1823-1906), Dutch
   playwright
1866 Georg II, Duke of Saxe-Meiningen
   (1826-1914) succeeds to throne
1871 German Empire founded

1874-1890 Meiningen Players tour world
1875
   Richard Wagner (1813-1883); Theory of
   Gesamtkunstwerk
Vienna's Burgtheater, major German-
   language theatre
1883 Theatrical reform initiated in
   Germany

1889-1894 Freie Bühne in Berlin;
   Otto Brahm (1856-1912), head

1896 Revolving stage installed in
   Residenz Theatre, Munich
Playwrights: Hermann Sudermann (1857-
1900 1928, Germany), Gerhart Hauptmann
   (1862-1946, Germany), Arthur
   Schnitzler (1862-1931, Austria),
   Maurice Maeterlinck (1862-1949,
   Belgium), Hugo von Hofmannsthal
   (1847-1929, Austria)
c. 1912 German Expressionism introduced
Max Reinhardt (1873-1943), theorist,
   director and producer

NORWAY, SWEDEN AND FINLAND

1850 National Norwegian Theatre
   opens in Bergen
1850 *Catilina,* Henrik Ibsen's (1828-
   1906) 1st published drama

1860 New Theatre dedicated in
   Helsinki

1865 *The Wedding at Ulfasa* by Frans
   Hedberg (1838-1908), Swedish
   playwright
1872 Finnish Theatre organized by
   Kaarlo Bergborn (1843-1906) and
   his sister Emilie (1834-1905)
1875 *A Bankruptcy* by Bjørnstjern
   Bjørnson (1832-1910), Norwegian
   playwright
August Strindberg (1849-1912)
Oskari Vilho (1840-1883), Father
   of Finnish Acting

1894 Swedish Domestic Theatre opens
   at Hanko
1899 National Theatre at Christiana
   (Oslo) opens
1902 Finland's National Theatre
   established

RUSSIA

1850 *A Month in the Country* by Ivan
Turgenev (1818-1883)
1853-1886 Active years of Alexander
Ostrovsky (1823-1886),
playwright

1866 Russian Society of Dramatic
Authors and Composers founded

1875 "Lines of business" abandoned
as basis of theatre employment
1876 1st permanent Yiddish theatre in
Russia established; Abraham
Goldfaden (1840-1908), founder
1886 *The Power of Darkness* by Leo
Tolstoy (1828-1910)
Other playwrights: Anton Chekhov
(1860-1904), Maxim Gorky (1868-
1936), Leonid Andreyev (1871-1919)
1892-1902 Troupe of N. N. Solovtsov
(1857-1902) plays Kiev and Odessa
1897 1st All-Russian Convention of
Theatrical Workers
1898 Moscow Art Theatre founded
1900 1902 *The Lower Depths* by Gorky
1904 *The Cherry Orchard* by Chekhov
1905 Russian Revolution
1907 *The Life of Man* by Andreyev
1909 Konstantin Stanislavsky (1863-
1938) outlines his "method of acting"
1910-1914 Vsevelod Meyerhold (1874-
1940) experiments with techniques
1914 Kamerny Theatre opens

LATIN AMERICA

1850 Gertrudis Gomez de Avellaneda
(1814-1873), Cuban playwright

1854 Center for Dramatic Authors
established in Colombia
Joaquim Manuel de Macedo (1820-1882),
Brazilian playwright
1862 *The Two Are Worse* by Isabel
Angel Prieto (1833-1876), Mexican
playwright
Other playwrights: Luis Rodriquez
Velasco (1838-1919, Chile), Pedro
Paz Soldari (1839-1895, Peru)
1868-1900 Cuban War of Independence
1869-1870 *Abdala* by José Marti (1853-
1895), Cuban freedom fighter

1885 *Don Lucas Gomez,* comedy, by
Mateo Martinez Quevedo (1848-
-1923), Chilean playwright
Playwrights: Antonio Mediz Bolio
(1884-1957, Mexico), Frederico
Gamboa (1864-1934, Mexico),
Nemesio Trejo (1862-1916, Argentina), Florencio Sanchez (1875-
1910, Uruguay), Alberto Vacarezza
(1888-1959, Argentina), Antonio
Alvarez Lluas (1892-1956, Colombia), Leopoldo Ayala Michelena
(1897-1962, Venezuela)
1902 Republic of Cuba established
Salesian priests in Argentina teach
through theatres ("*galpones* ")
1910 Sociedad de Fomento del Teatro
founded in Cuba
1915 Society of Chilean Playwrights

World Theatre, 1850-1915

THE UNITED STATES

1850
1852 Numerous productions of *Uncle Tom's Cabin*
1855 *Francesca da Rimini*, by George Henry Boker (1823-1896)
1856 Copyright Law enacted
Laura Keene (?-1873), theatre manager
1859 *The Octoroon*, by Dion Boucicault (1820-1890)

1861-1865 Civil War

1865 Lincoln assassinated at Ford's Theatre, Washington, D.C.
1865 *Rip Van Winkle* acted by Joseph Jefferson (1829-1905)
Augustin Daly (1836-1899), theatre entrepeneur
1975 Edwin Booth (1833-1893), actor
Edward Harrigan (1844-1908); Theatre Comique in New York
Steele Mackaye (1842-1894), playwright, actor, inventor
William Gillette (1855-1937), actor
1886 *The Old Homestead*, longest running American play, by Denman Thompson (1833-1911)
Bronson Howard (1842-1908), 1st professional playwright in U.S.A.
1890 *Margaret Fleming* by James A. Herne (1839-1901)
David Belasco (1853-1931), actor, playwright, manager
1896-1916 Theatrical Syndicate
1900 Clyde Fitch (1865-1909), playwright
1905 "47 Workshop"; George Pierce Baker (1866-1935) at Harvard
1909 *The Nigger* by Edward Sheldon (1866-1946)
Rachel Crothers (1878-1958), playwright
1910 Drama League of America founded
1915 The Provincetown Players organized

CANADA AND AUSTRALIA

1850 Westerners tour Australian theatres: Lola Montez (1818-1861), Madame Celeste (1814-1882), Dion Boucicault (1820-1890), Joseph Jefferson (1829-1905), Edwin Booth (1833-1893), Sarah Bernhardt (1844-1923)

Charles Heavysege (1816-1876), 1st Canadian verse playwright

1880-1914 Period of active theatre touring in Canada; mainly United States companies

1898 French Canadians show interest in French-language theatre
1903 *Les boules de neiges*, by Louvigny de Montigny, Canadian playwright

THE MIDDLE EAST AND AFRICA

• By the late 19th century Sub-Saharan Africa was being divided into "spheres of influence" by the major countries of the world at conferences where the African people were not represented.

• As Western travelers to the Middle East both viewed entertainments and brought their ideas to the area, Western drama influenced writers in Iran, Egypt and Turkey, while stimulating some playwrights to emphasize native themes. In Egypt the opening of the Suez Canal excited Ismail Pasha (1830-1895), Khedive, to build a *commedia* theatre and make Egypt, in his words, "a piece of Europe." A later Khedive supported the work of Jurj Abyad (1880-1962), whose troupes toured the Arabic world. In 1891 Khaili Al Kabbani (1836-1902) founded a theatre to produce folk plays in Egypt.

• Iran and Turkey experienced serious censorship problems until the early 20th century.

INDIA

• A major problem in tracing the history of modern theatre in India is the number of languages spoken in different parts of the country -- such as Hindustani, Hindi, Tegulu, Oriya, and English. Theatre in each state and each language has its own distinct beginning. This diversity makes a popular modern theatre extremely difficult to achieve in India.

• The Dramatic Performance Act of 1876 gave magistrates authority to stop any performance at any time and arrest the actors if the magistrate considered the play scandalous, defamatory in any way or having the potential to excite feelings of dissatisfaction with the government.

• Rabindranath Tagore (1861-1941) was the major modern playwright of India. Among his 50 plays is *The Post Office* (1913), which had a strong influence on the work of William Butler Yeats.

SOUTHEAST ASIA

• *Bangsawan* (the "noble people"), comparable to the *commedia dell'arte* and involving songs, skits and dance, was a popular entertainment for royalty and for state functions. The first professional troupe appeared in 1885. By 1902 other troupes were touring Malaysia and Indonesia.

• Particular origins of the very numerous musical, dance and dance-drama forms are virtually impossible to determine, and scholarly research to this end has only recently been undertaken. The *makyong* dance-drama of Malaysia probably goes back centuries as a harvest ritual. In modern times it was a court entertainment until 1920 and involved dialogue, music and dance. The enactment, in six parts, has a story line concerned with Pak Yong, a king, and Mak Yong, his queen. The *rangda-barong* dance-drama of Bali shows the evil, ugly spirit of Rangda and the benevolent spirit Barong. The Indonesian *ludruk besut* involves Buddhist-Hindu animistic rituals, an all-male cast and a story featuring Besut and the life cycle of man's birth, courtship, marriage, work and self-knowledge.

• A 1911 article in the journal of the Siam Society describes six theatre forms: *liki* was a clowning parody of Islamic recitations; *hun* was a show of contemporary stories presented by cylindrical marionettes; *nang* (no longer extant) were stories of Rama presented by transparent leather puppets; *lakon* was the recognized legitimate drama; *khon* was the mask drama; *manora* was the popular dance-drama of the woodsman who caught a fairy and the story of her love for Prince Suton.

CHINA

• Peking Operas are usually short plays with an emphasis upon warrior roles (*sheng*). Singing is a major aspect of the form. Orchestras are small; percussion instruments dominate, and strings support the voice. Actors wear special costumes involving a wide variety of headgear, robes and footwear which identify each character. Their make-up is elaborate, spectacular -- approximately 500 patterns -- and non-realistic. Actors use a variety of conventional gestures that are centuries old -- all supported by musical tempos -- and add to the sensational aspect of Peking Opera with acrobatics.

• Members of the Spring Willow Society staged their version of *Uncle Tom's Cabin,* called *The Negro Slave Sighs to Heaven,* in Shanghai in 1907. Other drama societies -- the Sun of Springtime Society (1909) in Peking, the Progressive Society (1910-1912) in Shanghai -- produced plays featuring plot, dialogue and Western style staging and scenery.

JAPAN AND KOREA

• The change from shogunate rule to that of the Emperor Meiji (1868) brought Japan into the modern world. *Shinsei shimpa* eschewed political content, avoided imitating Western drama, as well as the melodramatic sensationalism of the older *shimpa,* and concentrated on contemporary Meiji issues. Actors wore Meiji costumes. This was the first modern theatre form distinct from *kabuki* to become established in Japan. As *shinsei shimpa* became popular, *kabuki* declined.

• Political problems in Korea weakened and adulterated progress in the theatre, but Koreans became interested in the Japanese *shimpa.* Yi In-Jig (1861-1916), a political exile in Japan from 1884 to 1894, wrote *The Silver World* (1908) which was produced at the National Theatre in Seoul and is considered to mark the beginning of modern drama in Korea.

World Theatre, 1850-1915

ITALY AND SPAIN

• In Spanish drama Romanticism gave way to the pseudo-realism of the *alta comedia*, which presented contemporary society in a realistic manner. The general critical attitude toward theatre was so questioning that the Nobel Prize awarded to José Echegaray (1832-1916) was protested by members of the "Generation of 1898." Although Jacinto Benavente (1866-1954) dominated Spanish drama during the early 20th century, he was unable to place Spanish theatre in the mainstream of American and European theatre.

• There were no dramas of consequence written in late 19th century Italy and little activity in Italian theatres. Touring stars -- Adelaide Ristori (1822-1906) and Tommaso Salvini (1829-1915), for example -- provided the major attraction. After the turn of the century, playwrights still failed to be innovative, while actors like Eleanora Duse (1859-1924) continued Italy's acting traditions.

FRANCE

• French drama during the last part of the 19th century was generally popular and slight, written to fill the numerous Parisian theatres. Between 1860 and 1900 Eugene Labiche (1815-1888) and Victorien Sardou (1831-1908) satisfied theatregoers.

• French theatre of the late 19th and early 20th centuries made particular contributions to world theatre through the commentary of Emile Zola (1849-1902), the plays of Henri Becque (1837-1899) and the experimentation within André Antoine's Théâtre Libre, the Théâtre d'Art of Paul Forte (1872-1962) and the Théâtre l'Oeuvre of Aurelien-Marie Lugne-Poë (1869-1940).

• One of the first theorists interested in non-illusionistic theatre design, Adolphe Appia (1862-1928) recommended three-dimensional stage units, the use of light related to music and mood and a unity of artistic approach to production demanding the authority of a strong director.

• The ideas of Jacques Copeau (1879-1949) as revealed in his Théâtre du Vieux Colombier promoted the importance of the playwright. His season of 1913-1914 was particularly impressive, but World War I brought a halt to his work which, after the war, would dominate French theatre.

ENGLAND AND IRELAND

• During most of the 19th century British drama was unimpressive, to be rescued from its unenviable existence by one who is quoted as saying that the drama was always at a "low ebb": George Bernard Shaw (1856-1950). Before Shaw appeared, writers of melodrama and burlesque entertained audiences -- with only one playwright of note, Thomas W. Robertson (1829-1871) -- until Gilbert and Sullivan began writing. Oscar Wilde (1856-1900) made his reputation with comedies of wit and elegance such as *The Importance of Being Earnest* (1895).

• English theatre of this period is memorable for its actor-managers and such theatre managers as Charles Fechter (1824-1876), Squire Bancroft (1841-1926) and Mrs. Marie Effie Bancroft (1839-1921) . Henry Irving (1838-1905) exerted the most influence as an actor -- with Ellen Terry (1847-1928), his leading lady -- and as manager of the Lyceum Theatre (1878-1898). After Irving, Herbert Beerbohm Tree (1853-1917) was the most famous English actor-manager until 1914.

• After 1900 Irish theatre was clearly established through the efforts of Lady Gregory (1863-1935) and William Butler Yeats (1865-1939). Their association with the Abbey Theatre helped bring its reputation for exceptional ensemble acting to international attention. John Millington Synge (1871-1909) added to the reputation of the Abbey with such plays as *Riders to the Sea* (1904).

GERMANY AND CENTRAL EUROPE

• Through the Meiningen Players the Duke of Saxe-Meiningen emphasized a complete illusion on the stage and an authoritarian approach which caused this to occur. Richard Wagner (1813-1883) also insisted upon a single authority to fuse all parts of a production into a *gesamtkunstwerk*. Both men exerted strong influence upon modern theories of directing.

• The Freie Bühne, headed by Otto Brahm (1856-1912) and dedicated to Realism and Naturalism, offered an opportunity for new playwrights, such as Gerhart Hauptmann (1862-1946) with *The Weavers* (1892), but had little effect upon production practice. In 1894 Brahm became director of Deutsches Theater. In 1905, as Brahm's successor at the Deutsches Theater, Max Reinhardt (1873-1943) practiced the theories and performed the experimentation that would affect all German theatre.

• Playwrights of the period include Austrian Arthur Schnitzler (1862-1931) with *The Lonely Way* (1904) and Hugo von Hofmannsthal (1874-1929). Maurice Maeterlinck (1862-1949), the Belgian symbolist, wrote *The Blue Bird* (1909). In the Netherlands an early playwright, Hendrich Jan Schimmel (1823-1906) was supported by the Royal Association of the Dutch Stage, which he headed, and Marcellus Emants (1848-1923), criticized the Durch bourgeoisie in such plays as *The Power of Sympathy* (1904).

• Expressionism is a non-realistic style of theatre and drama in which the artist projects attitudes of mind and emotion through distortion, exaggeration and mechanical movements. It is a highly subjective approach in which events and people are frequently seen through the eyes of the protagonist. The first German expressionistic play was *The Beggar* (1912) by Reinhard Johannes Sorge (1892-1916).

World Theatre, 1850-1915

NORWAY, SWEDEN AND FINLAND

• A mildly active, if not innovative, theatre existed in all three countries during this period. For many scholars the first publication of an Ibsen play, *Catilina* (1850), marks the beginning of modern drama in the Western world. The contributions of Henrik Ibsen (1828-1906) and August Strindberg (1849-1912) outshone any of their national contemporaries as well as most of the playwrights writing in any language in the world. Ibsen's plays include *Brand* (1865), *Peer Gynt* (1867), *A Doll's House* (1879), *Ghosts* (1881), *The Lady from the Sea* (1888), *Hedda Gabler* (1890) and *When We Dead Awaken* (1999). Among Strindberg's plays are *The Father* (1887), *Miss Julie* (1888), *To Damascus* (1898) and *A Dream Play* (1902).

• Frans Hedberg's (1838-1908) play, *The Wedding at Ulfasa*, was one of the most popular at the time, and Bjørnstjerne Bjørnson (1832-1910) also enjoyed a fair reputation among theatregoers.

RUSSIA

• Russia was changing during the third quarter of the 19th century and with it the theatres and the plays presented there. Plays by Ivan Turgenev (1818-1883) and Alexander Ostrovsky (1823-1886) showed a distinctively Russian people. Imperial theatre monopolies were stopped; companies toured beyond Moscow and St. Petersburg; and a visit from the Meiningen Players in 1880 stimulated theatre artists. The trend toward Realism, however, moved slowly.

• Only with the formation of the Moscow Art Theatre in 1898 by Konstantin Stanislavsky (1863-1938) and Vladimir Nemirovich-Danchenko (1855-1943), was the theatre of Russia prepared to produce the plays of Anton Chekhov (1860-1904) and Maxim Gorky (1868-1936). At the same time, there were revolts against Realism which was first mentioned in 1898 in a journal, *The World of Arts*, edited by Sergei Diaghilev (1872-1929). One of the experimentors was Vsevelod Meyerhold (1874-1940). Realistic playwright Leonid Andreyev (1871-1919) converted to Symbolism and wrote *The Life of Man* (1907).

• Chekhov's major plays include *The Seagull* (1896), *Uncle Vanya* (1899), *The Three Sisters* (1901) and *The Cherry Orchard* (1904) -- all of which were staged by Stanislavsky at the Moscow Art Theatre -- and numerous one-act farces such as *The Bear* (1888).

LATIN AMERICA

• Many countries of South America had not yet established native theatres of substance during this period -- Paraguay, Venezuela and Ecuador, for example. For this entire period Chilean theatre was dominated by popular writers of brief comedies such as Luis Rodriquez

Velasco (1838-1919). Peruvian theatre also emphasized comedy, as in the plays of Pedro Paz Soldari (1839-1895). Theatres in Brazil emphasized light farce and musical comedy until the end of the 19th century. No country in Central America could boast a vital theatre during these years.

• Only a few countries followed the trends of Europe -- Mexico, Argentina and Colombia. In Uruguay attitudes began to change with the plays of Victor Pérez Petit (1871-1947) and Florencio Sanchez (1875-1910). A more realistic approach to art stimulated critics to consider Antonio Alvarez Lluas (1892-1956) Colombia's best playwright.

• Cuban playwrights endured the long seige for independence during which the theatre world progressed from Neoclassicism to Romanticism to Realism. Popular comedy sustained audiences at the Alhambra Theatre, whereas the Sociedad de Fomento del Teatro, founded in 1910, had a distinct goal: to create a new theatre.

THE UNITED STATES

• This was a period during which Americans took control of their theatres from English managers, created a core of actors and produced playwrights who could make a good living.

• Most of the theatre managers were also actors and/or playwrights. Laura Keene (?-1873) was the most successful woman manager of her time in America. Dion Boucicault (1820-1890) contributed to American drama, had a hand in passing the first American copyright law affecting playwrights and wrote a series of critical essays for the *North American Review*. Augustin Daly (1836-1899) wrote popular melodrama (*Under the Gaslight*, 1867), managed several theatres and toured American troupes in England and on the Continent. Edward Harrigan (1844-1908) teamed up with Tony Hart (1855-1891) at his Theatre Comique in New York with exceptional success in his own Mulligan Guard plays. Steele Mackaye (1842-1894) combined playwriting skills (*Hazel Kirke*, 1880) with a genius for invention.

• In 1896 six men (Sam Nixon, Fred Zimmerman, Charles Frohman, Al Hayman, Marc Klaw and Abe Erlanger) attempted to gain control of the American theatre through the booking agencies for theatres, actors and playwrights, thus forming the Theatrical Syndicate. Other empressarios, such as the Shubert Brothers, competed, and the last Syndicate contract was signed in 1916.

• Edwin Booth (1833-1893) brought distinction to American acting, as did Augustin Daly with his interest in ensemble acting and his insistence upon control of his company, reflected the policies of European theatres. The career William Gillette (1855-1937) illustrates the "matinee idol" in such plays as his own *Secret Service* (1895).

• *The Old Homestead* (1886), born a decade earlier as the skit, *Joshua Whitcomb*, was acted by Denman Thompson (1833-1911) until his death. Bronson Howard (1842-1908), the first American to make his living as a playwright, wrote *The Young Mrs. Winthrop* (1882) and other plays. With *Margaret Fleming* (1890), James A. Herne (1839-1901) marked a new direction toward Realism, and Clyde Fitch (1865-1909) was the first millionaire playwright. George Jean Nathan, American critic, called Edward Sheldon's *The Nigger* (1909) the most important play of the 20th century.

CANADA AND AUSTRALIA

• English-language theatre in Canada developed slowly as troupes from the United States toured Canadian cities, and New York drew Canadian writers as a theatre center. Interest in French-language theatre was spurred by activity in Montreal and Quebec and by the erection of new theatres in other eastern locations.

• During this entire period Australia was a popular place for touring stars from England and America.

World Theatre, 1916-1945

THE MIDDLE EAST AND AFRICA

1916 1917 Habimah Theatre founded
1918 Ottoman Empire ends
c. 1918 Komedi-e Theatre founded in
  Iran; Ali Nasr (1893-1965), founder
1919-1945 Trusteeships in Africa
Ahmad Shauqui (1868-1932),
  Egyptian playwright
1920 *The Dybbuk* by S. Anski (1863-1920)
  staged by Vilna Theatre in Russia
1923 Republic of Turkey established
1923-1938 Ataturk Westernizes Turkey
Naquib Al-Rihani (1892-1949),
  Egyptian playwright
Turkish playwrights: Ibnirrefils
  Ahmet Nuri (1874-1935),
  Musahipzade Celal (1870-1959)
1925 Ohel Theatre (Israeli Labor
  Theatre) founded in Tel Aviv
1925-1941 Censorship in Iran

1930 1930's 500 community theatres built
  in Turkey
Tawfiq Al-Hakim (1898-1987), Father
  of Modern Egyptian Drama
Mattathais Shoham (1893-1936),
  Hebrew playwright

1936 State Conservatory for Music
  and Drama founded in Turkey

1944 Cameri Theatre founded in
  Tel Aviv
Iranian playwrights: Mortezaqoli
  Fekri (1868-1917), Mirzâdeh Eshqi
  (1893-1925), Sâdeq Hedâvat (1903-
  1951)

INDIA AND SOUTHEAST ASIA

1920-1935 Golden Age of *Bangsawan*
  in Malaysia
1920-1945 *Pya zat* (modern play) of
  Burma
1920's Elements of Realism introduced
  throughout India
1920's *Sandiwara*, popular local or
  historical tales in Sunda
1920's *Ludruk besutan* in Indonesia
1920's More than 200 theatre
  companies founded in Gujarat
1924 *Red Oleanders* by Rabindranath
  Tagore (1861-1941)
1920's-1933 Growth of Hindi-language
  theatre in India
1930's Decline of Parsi theatre in India
1930's Professional theatre companies
  organized in Orisia, India
Indian playwrights: Jai Shankar
  Prasad (1889-1937), Jyoti Prasad
  Agarwala (1903-1951)
1932 Constitutional Monarchy in Siam
1934 Siamese government Department
  of Fine Arts sponsors theatre

Late 1930's Popularity of the
  People's Theatre in India
1940-1942 Japan invades Siam,
  Malaysia and Indonesia and uses
  ludruk for propaganda
1944 *New Harvest* by Bijon
  Bhattacharya begins new theatre
  in Bengal

World Theatre, 1916-1945

CHINA

1916
   1917 "New Culture" movement promotes
      "spoken drama"
   1918 Issue of *New Youth* journal devoted
      to Ibsen
   1918-1920   33 Western plays translated
      into Chinese
   1919 May 4th Movement
   1921 Communist Party in China
   1921 Creation Society founded in Shanghai
   1922 1st issue of *Creation Quarterly*
      includes play by Tien Han (1896-1968)
   Chinese playwrights: Hung Shen (1893-
      1955), Ouyang Yu-chien (1889-1962),
      Kuo Mo-jo (1892-1978), Hsiung Fo-hsi
      (1900-1965)
   1926-1949 Chiang Kai-shek (Kuomintang)
      vs. Mao Tse-tung (Communists)
   1928 South China Society for theatre
      training founded
1930
   1931 League of Left-Wing Dramatists
      founded
   1931 Communist Workers and Peasants
      Dramatic Society founded
   1934 China Traveling Dramatic Troupes
   1934-1935 Long March of Mao Tse-tung
   1934-1941 Influential work of Ts'ao Yu
      (1910-), Father of Modern Chinese
      Drama
   1935 Nanjing National Academy
      of Dramatic Art founded
   1937 Japan invades China
   1937 National Dramatic Association
      to Resist the Enemy founded

   1942 Mao Tse-tung's *Talks at the Yenan
      Forum on Literature and Art*

JAPAN AND KOREA

Japan rules Korea until 1945
Hyon Chul (1891-1965) founds
   Academy of Arts in Korea

1920's Mainly left-wing theatre
   in Japan
1921 *Shinguk,* realistic Western
   drama, introduced to Korea
1922 Communist Party in Japan
1922 Earth and Moon Society in
   Korea produces Western plays
1924-1928 Tsukiji Little Theatre
   founded in Japan
1925 Communist Party in Korea
Ito Kisaku (1899-1967), Japanese
   designer

1930 Federation of Korean Proletarian Art includes drama
1931-1939 Theatre Arts Research
   Society in Korea
1932 Japan attacks China
1930's Approximately 100
   commercial and experimental
   theatre groups in Korea
1930's 3 Japanese *shingeki*
   companies operate
Shimpa and *kabuki* continue
Japanese playwrights: Kubo
   Sahae (1900-1957), Kishida
   Kunio (1890-1954)
1937 Japanese government
   suppresses all political theatre
1940 Japanese government dissolves
   reactionary theatre troupes
1941 Japan attacks Pearl Harbor
1941 Japanese police try to force
   Korean playwrights to glorify
   Japan

World Theatre, 1916-1945

ITALY AND SPAIN

1916 Theatre of the Grotesque in Italy

1920's Popularity of Futurism in Italy
1922 Mussolini takes power in Italy
Esperpento developed by Ramón del Valle-Inclan (1869-1936), Spanish playwright
Luigi Pirandello (1876-1936), Italian playwright
Anton Guilio Bragaglia (1890-1960), Italian playwright

1929-1940's State support of *carri di tespi* (mobile theatre) in Italy
1930
1932 La Barraca theatre founded in Spain

Spanish playwrights: Ramón del Valle-Inclán (1869-1936), Federico García Lorca (1899-1936), Alejandro Casona (1903-1966)

1935 Accademia d'Arte Drammatica founded in Rome
1936-1939 Civil War in Spain

1943 Italy declares war on Germany

FRANCE AND CENTRAL EUROPE

Jacques Copeau (1879-1949), actor-director

1920 Théâtre National Populaire founded
1920-1929 Jacques Copeau's School
August Defresne (1893-1961), Dutch playwright
Michel de Ghelderode (1892-1962), Belgian playwright

1927 Formation of the Cartel: Louis Jouvet (1887-1951), Charles Dullin (1885-1949), Georges Pitöeff (1884-1939), Gaston Baty (1882-1951)
Jean Cocteau (1889-1963), French surrealistic playwright
Sacha Guitry (1885-1957) writes, directs and acts in about 150 plays
1930 Compaigne des Quinze
1930's "Lay plays" flourish in Netherlands

1938 *The Theatre and Its Double* by Antoin Artaud (1896-1949), French visionary
French playwrights: André Obey (1892-1975), Jean Giraudoux (1882-1944), Jean Anouilh (1910-1987)
1940 Germany invades France

1944 Allies liberate France

World Theatre, 1916-1945

ENGLAND AND IRELAND

1916
  1918-1928 Dublin Drama League
  1919 British Drama League founded
  1919 Little theatre movement
    flourishes in England; actor-
    manager system disappears
  1923 *St. Joan*, Shaw's last success
  1925 Gate Theatre opens in London
  1928 Gate Theatre founded in Dublin

  Irish playwrights: Sean O'Casey
    (1880-1964), William Butler
    Yeats (1865-1939), Denis Johnston
    (1901-1984)

1930 1931 Mercury Theatre opens
    in London
  English actors: Sybil Thorndike
    (1882-1976), Edith Evans
    1976), John Gielgud (1904-)
  English playwrights: Somerset
    Maugham (1874-1965), Emlyn
    Williams (1905-1987, Wales),
    T. S. Eliot (1888-1965)

  1939 England declares war on
    Axix powers
  1939 Old Vic closes because of
    war

GERMANY AND EASTERN EUROPE

1914-1918 World War I
1916 *From Morn to Midnight* by Georg
  Kaiser (1878-1945), German
  playwright
1918 Salzburg Festival established
1918-1939 An independent Poland
  stimulates theatre activity
1919 Leopold Jessner (1878-1945),
  director of Berlin State Theatre
1919 The Bauhaus established by
  Walter Gropius (1883-1969)
1922 Max Reinhardt (1873-1943),
  director of Vienna's Redoutensad
  Theatre
1923 Rise of *Neue Sachlichkeit*
  in Germany
1927 Vest Pocket Revue, improvised
  theatre in Czechoslovakia
1927 Piscator Theatre founded in
  Germany

1933 Rise of Adolf Hitler
Epic Theatre of Bertolt Brecht (1898-
  1956)
Major playwrights: Ernst Toller (1893-
  1939, Germany), Carl Zuckmayer
  (1896-1977, Germany), Franz
  Werfel (1890-1945, Austria), Karel
  Capek (1890-1938, Czechoslovakia),
  Ferenc Molnar (1878-1952, Hungary),
  Stanislaw Ignacy Witkiewicz
  (1885-1939, Poland)

World Theatre, 1916-1945

SCANDINAVIA

1916 Swedish-speaking National
Theatre established in Finland

1917 Finnish Civil War; Finland
becomes a republic in 1919

1917 Betty Nansen Theatre opens in
Copenhagen

1918 *Modern Theatre: Points of View
and Attack* by Pär Lagerkvist
(1889-1974), Swedish playwright

1922 Trondelag Teater opens in
Trondheim, Norway

1920's-1930's Strindberg Renaissance;
interpretations of Swedish
director Per Lindberg (1896-1944)

Swedish playwrights: Hjalmar
Bergman (1883-1931), Wilhelm
Moberg (1888-1973)

Norwegian playwrights: Oskar
Braathen (1881-1939), Nordahl
Grieg (1902-1943)

1930

1930's Experimental productions in
Denmark

Danish playwrights: Kaj Munk
(1898-1944), Kjeld Abell (1901-
1961)

Language conflict in Finland

Finnish playwrights: Maria
Lotuni (1880-1943), Lauri
Haarla (1890-1944)

1939 Soviet Union invades
Finland

1940 Germany invades Norway

1940 Germany occupies Denmark

THE SOVIET UNION

1917 Russian Revolution

1918-1925 Professional and amateur
theatre encouraged

1920 Vsevolod Meyerhold (1874-
1940) becomes director of all
theatre

Vevgemy Vokhtangov (1883-1922),
innovative director

1923-1924 Moscow Art Theatre tours
America

1924-1936 2nd Moscow Art Theatre;
Mikhail Chekhov (1891-1955),
director

1927 Realistic Theatre established

1927-1945 Russian theatre subject to
propaganda of Socialist Realism

Playwrights: Vladimir Mayakovsky
(1894-1930), Mikhail Bulgakov
(1891-1940), Nikolai Pogodin
(1900-1962), Alexander Afinogenov
(1904-1941)

1932 Maxim Gorky (1868-1936) heads
Union of Soviet Writers

1936 All theatres placed under
Central Direction of Theatres

1941 Germany invades Soviet Union

1943 Aleksandr Tairov (1885-1950)
heads Theatre of the Revolution

World Theatre, 1916-1945

LATIN AMERICA AND THE CARIBBEAN

1916
1917 1st theatre in Santiago, Chile
1920's Paragon Players of Port-of-Spain, Trinidad
1921 Teatro Folklorico established in Mexico
1924 Teatro del Murciélago founded in Mexico
1924 Colmeia, theatre reform group in Brazil
1925 Grupo de los Siete Autores founded in Mexico
1925-1926 National Dramatic Company founded in Quito
1928-1947 Experimental theatre groups in Mexico
1920's-1930's Chilean theatre resists reform
1929 "Theatre for the Masses" opens in Jamaica
1930   Independent theatre movement in Argentina
Luis Enrique Osorio (1896-1966), Colombian playwright
Rodolfo Usigli (1905-1979), Mexican author of 40 plays
1936 Teatro la Cueva company of Luis A. Baralt in Cuba
1938 The Comedians of Brazil, experimental theatre
1938 Association of Amateur Artists in Peru advances drama
1941 Little Theatre Movement in Jamaica
1941 Teatro Experimental de la Universidad de Chile founded
1942-1947 Society of Friends of Theatre in Venezuela
1943-1945 Teatro Popular in Cuba
1943 Production of *Bridal Gown* by Nelson Rodriques (1912-1981); modern drama begins in Brazil

THE UNITED STATES

1915-1929 The Provincetown Players; Eugene O'Neill (1888-1953)
1917 *Why Marry?*, 1st Pulitzer Prize play, by J. L. Williams (1871-1929)
1918 Theatre Guild formed
1918 United Scenic Artists established
1919 Actor's Equity Association recognized
Scenic designers: Robert Edmond Jones (1887-1959), Lee Simonson (1888-1967), Norman Bel Geddes (1893-1958)
1926-1932 Civic Repertory Theatre; Eva LeGallienne (1899-1991), head
1927-1928   280 plays produced at 80 theatres during New York season

1929 Stock Market Crash

1931-1941 Group Theatre
1930's Left-wing theatres: Theatre Union (1933-1937), League of Workers' Theatre (1932-1934)
1935-1939 Federal Theatre Project: Living Newspapers, Negro Theatre Unit
Playwrights: Elmer Rice (1892-1967), Maxwell Anderson (1888-1959), Robert Sherwood (1896-1955), George S. Kaufman (1889-1962), Langston Hughes (1902-1967), Clifford Odets (1906-1963), Lillian Hellman (1906-1964), Thornton Wilder (1897-1975)
1930's -1940's Negro theatre
1938-1960 The Playwrights' Company
1939 *Life with Father* by Lindsay and Crouse breaks long run record
1941 United States enters WW II
1943 *Oklahoma!*

World Theatre, 1916-1945

CANADA

1916 Merrill Denison (1893-1975),
Canada's 1st important English-
language playwright
1919 Hart House Theatre formed
in Toronto as focus of little
theatre movement
1921 Community Players organized
in Montreal

1930 Left-wing theatres: Theatre of
Action, Workers' Theatre
1930's French-speaking radio
theatre, largely in Quebec
1932 Dominion Drama Festival
formed for amateur production

English-language playwrights:
John Coulter (1888-1980),
Robertson Davies (1913-),
Gwen Pharis Ringwood (1910-
1984)

French-language playwrights:
Gustave Lamarche (b. 1925),
Rose Ouellette (b. 1903)

AUSTRALIA

1922-1926 Pioneer Players,
Melbourne, co-founded by
Louis Esson (1879-1943),
Australia's 1st realistic play-
wright; *The Drovers* (1923),
Shipwreck (1928)
1922-1931 The Pioneer Players
in Sydney
Other playwrights: Oriel Gray,
Sydney Tomholt

1930-1974 Independent Theatre in
Sydney
1930 Community Players organized
in Sydney
1930's Left-wing theatre in several
Australian cities
1930's Outback theatre movement:
Katherine S. Prichard's *Brumly
Innes* (1927), Bernard Cronin's
Stampede (1937)

World Theatre, 1916-1945

THE MIDDLE EAST

• Founded in Moscow in 1917 by Nahum Zemach (1887-1939), the Habimah Theatre was to perform plays in Hebrew. With the production of S. Ansky's *The Dybbuk* in 1922, it won international acclaim. During extensive world tours the theatre experienced particular difficulties in America in 1927, when the actors split: some stayed in America; some returned to Europe. In 1932 the company settled in Tel Aviv, moved into its own theatre in 1945 and was declared the Israeli National Theatre in 1958.

• Prior to World War I the Ottoman Empire ruled territory that now comprises Syria, Lebanon, Iraq, Iran, Jordan, Israel, Saudi Arabia and Yemen. With the establishment of the Republic under Ataturk, Turkey established regional theatres, set up state theatres and state operas during the 1940's and supported playwrights.

• Iranian theatre experienced severe censorship under the rule of Reza Shah Pahlavi from 1925 to 1941, during which no socio-political allusions were allowed in the plays. Sâdeq Hedâyat (1903-1951) wrote historical plays to avoid censorship; the patriot poet Mirzâdeh Eshqi (1893-1925) wrote six plays.

• In Egypt Ahmad Shauqi (1868-1932) wrote six historical plays and one comedy. Naquib Al-Rihani (1892-1949) was most popular for his creation of Kish Kish Bey, a pompous rural bureaucrat who became the object and purveyor of satire. Tawfiq Al-Hakim (1898-1987) is now considered the Father of Modern Egyptian Drama, primarily for plays written after 1945. His first produced play, *People of the Cave* (1933), gained him a reputation, as did *The Tree of Power* (1943), in which he ridiculed Egyptian bureaucracy.

INDIA AND SOUTHEAST ASIA

• *Bangsawan* was the first Malaysian theatre form to use the proscenium stage. Like *commedia dell'arte* it follows no script and the play depends upon the skills of the actors: a heroine, a hero (*Orang Muda*), a clown or two and a demon or genie. Every *bangsawan* troupe (consisting of 15-30 men and women) carries a set of six drops: interior of a palace, a street scene, a jungle, a garden, interior of a poor man's home and a landscape. Costumes and make-up are stock. An orchestra accompanies the performance, which can include classical tories or versions of Shakespeare.

• Realism from Western drama came to India during the 1920's and spread throughout the country into the different language-speaking theatres. As the Parsi theatre around Bombay declined in popularity, a shift occurred from themes involving myth and history to plays of social realistic themes which were written by playwrights in most parts of India.

• Traditional Indonesian *ludruk* changed about 1920 from the clown and the female impersonator to become *ludruk besutan,* in which the clown acquired a wife and the wife, an uncle. Later, a wealthy man was added, and the form became *ludruk besep.* During the 1930's troupes were organized by Tjak Gondo Durasim (d. 1944) and became sufficiently potent theatre to be banned by the Dutch in 1936. Structurally, a performance lasted about four and a half hours and was divided into four parts: an opening dance, songs and dances by the clown, songs and dances by the female impersonator and a melodramatic story.

• The People's Theatre was a politically oriented theatre in India which began in the late 1930's -- as part of the Progressive Writers' Association, spurred by the anti-Fascist movement -- and would continue to grow.

CHINA

• With the "New Culture" movement of 1917, Western drama -- particularly the works of Henrik Ibsen, such as *A Doll's House* -- became a major influence. The May 4th Movement of 1919 allowed the vernacular to be accepted in the theatre, and new translations of Western plays promoted the establishment during the 1920's of several societies dedicated to changes in literature and theatre. Eventually, all playwrights were forced to bow to the policies of Mao Tse-tung.

• With few exceptions, all plays written between about 1928 and 1949 were part of the ongoing policy that Art Serves Politics, and both Chiang Kia-shek and Mao Tse-tung used the theatre to promote their political ends. Mao's *Talks at the Yenan Forum* makes his philosophy clear: drama is a weapon.

• The single exception to the political drama of the period were the plays of Ts'ao Yu (1910-) during the 1930's. *Thunderstorm* (1934), his first play, is usually considered his best. Other titles include *Sunrise* (1936), *Wilderness* (1937) and *Peking Man* (1940). All show his admiration for Western literature, from the Greeks through Shakespeare to the plays of Ibsen and Eugene O'Neill.

JAPAN AND KOREA

• These were difficult years for Japanese theatre. As *shimpa* and *kabuki* troupes continued, Western drama infiltrated via *shingeki* companies such as the Tsukiji Little Theatre (1924-1928), founded by Hijikata Yoshi (1898-1959) to promote Western drama and plays that were realistic and generally left-wing. Although the popular left-wing emphasis of the 1920's was suppressed by the 1930's and then banned, the influence of Kubo Sakae (1900-1957) and Kishida Kunio (1890-1954) remained. In 1932 Kishida founded *Gekisaku* (Playwriting), a magazine which influenced the work of other writers.

• Like Japan, Korea was influenced by Western Realism and socialist thought throughout the 1920's, and, while a number of experimental theatre groups were active during the 1930's, no great plays resulted. The country was under the control of Japan, whose police did not tolerate subversive activity: after only 40 productions, the Tangewhoe Society, headed by Kim U-jin (1897-1927), was abolished; the Theatre Arts Research Society, which presented Western as well as original Korean plays, was closed in 1939.

ITALY AND SPAIN

• In Italy the Theatre of the Grotesque took its inspiration and its name from *The Mask and the Face* (1916) by Luigi Chiarelli (1884-1947), who, with others, was attempting to revitalize the Italian theatre. Futurism had little effect upon the theatre, where the major exponent was Enrico Prampolini (1894-1960).

• The single outstanding Italian dramatist was Luigi Pirandello (1867-1936), who wrote his best plays during the 1920's and 1930's: *Six Characters in Search of an Author* (1921), *Enrico IV* (1922) and *To Find Oneself* (1932). From 1924 to 1928, Pirandello headed the Art Theatre of Rome.

• In spite of Mussolini's warring activity throughout this period -- in Ethiopia, Spain and Germany -- he supported and encouraged theatres such as the Teatro degli Independenti in Rome, led by Anton Bragaglia (1890-1960) from 1922 to 1936, as well as the "noble theatres" which toured the provinces. By the 1930's, however, censorship was also a factor.

• In Spain Federico García Lorca (1899-1936) worked with La Barraca theatre group and developed a poetic tragedy which remains an outstanding contribution to that genre: *Blood Wedding* (1933) and *The House of Bernarda Alba* (1936). A lesser playwright, Alejandro Casona (1903-1966), worked with the government sponsored People's Theatre and fled Spain in 1936.

• Spanish playwright Jacinto Benavente (1866-1954) continued his popular success. Ramón del Valle-Inclán (1869-1936) wrote biting satires and was innovative with his concept of *esperpento*, which he described as a distortion of the norms of theatre and illustrated with *Lights of Bohemia* (1920).

FRANCE AND CENTRAL EUROPE

• Theatrical innovations dominated much of this period. Firmin Gémier (1869-1933), director of the Odeon from 1920 to 1930, persuaded the government to create the Théâtre National Populaire in 1920. A visionary of the avant garde, Antoin Artaud (1896-1948) founded the non-realistic theatre, the Théâtre Alfred Jarry, in 1926. Jacques Copeau's (1879-1949), ideas were a strong influence on Louis Jouvet (1887-1951), who teamed up with three others in 1927 to form the Cartel. Other students of Copeau, among them Michel Saint-Denis (1897-1971), formed the Compaigne des Quinze in 1930.

• Like Maeterlinck, Michel de Ghelderode (1898-1962) was a Fleming who wrote in French.

His plays, such as *Pantagleize* (1929), show powerful conflicts between tragedy and farce. His works did not gain wide recognition, however, until after World War II.

• Among French playwrights, Jean Cocteau (1892-1963) showed his surrealistic wit in such theatre works as *Parade* (1917), a ballet composed in collaboration with Pablo Picasso, and his personal approach in *The Infernal Machine* (1934). While Jean Anouilh (1910-1987) was beginning his career with such plays as *Carnival of Thieves* (1938) and *Antigone* (1943), Jean Giraudoux (1882-1944) ended his with a posthumous production of *The Madwoman of Chaillot* in 1945, staged by Jouvet.

• The "lay plays" from the Netherlands were serious plays by non-professional play-wrights writing for a coterie audience.

ENGLAND AND IRELAND

• English theatre changed markedly after World War I. Production methods changed; the Little Theatre Movement spread across the country; new theatres opened; repertory companies appeared outside London. The Old Vic, having produced Shakespeare during the war years under Ben Greet (1857-1936), acquired the Sadler's Wells Theatre in 1931 and, largely under the guidance of Tyrone Guthrie (1900-1971), became the most respected theatre in England by 1939.

• All things did not run smoothly at Dublin's Abbey Theatre. Denis Johnston's (1901-1984) first play was rejected, and Sean O'Casey (1880-1964) left after the management refused to produce *The Silver Tassie* in 1928, although *Juno and the Paycock* (1924) had been a great success. William Butler Yeats (1865-1939), Nobel Prize winner in 1923, however, continued to write lyrical and experimental plays such as *At the Hawk's Well* (1916) and *The Dreaming of the Bones* (1931).

• Among the popular English playwrights of this period were Somerset Maugham (1874-1965) with *The Circle* (1921), Emlyn Williams (1905-1987) with *The Corn Is Green* (1938) and Noel Coward (1899-1973) with *Private Lives* (1930) and *Blithe Spirit* (1941). Only T.S. Eliot (1888-1965), the American-born Englishman, would maintain a career -- well established with *Murder in the Cathedral* (1935) -- beyond the period.

GERMANY AND EASTERN EUROPE

• Georg Kaiser's (1878-1945) *From Morn to Midnight* (1916) became the major example of German expressionistic drama. Max Reinhardt (1873-1943) continued his work in Austria and Germany as the premier expressionistic director of the period.

• The neorealism of the *Neue Sachlichkist* is well illustrated by Carl Zuchmayer (1896-1977) in *The Captain of Kopenich* (1931).

• Attempting to create a proletarian drama, Erwin Piscator (1893-1966) prepared the way for Epic Theatre, a form connected with Bertolt Brecht (1898-1956). In *The Three-Penny Opera* (1928), *Mother Courage* (1937) and *The Caucasian Chalk Circle* (1944-1945), Brecht promoted his "theories of alienation," in which he sought a thoughtful and critical contemplation of a play by the audience.

SCANDINAVIA

• Sweden had the most active theatre in Scandinavia at this time, as Pär Lagerkvist (1889-1974) stimulated a reassessment of Strindberg's work with *Modern Theatre: Points of View and Attack* (1918). Two of Lagerkvist's own popular works were *The Hangman* (1933) and *Man Without a Soul* (1936). Per Lindberg (1896-1944) produced the major works of Strindberg and Lagerkvist.

• Theatre activity in Norway tended to take place in the National Theatre, but smaller theatres were being established. Oskar Braathen (1881-1939) wrote largely working-class plays; Nordahl Grieg (1902-1943) followed the dominant realistic traditions with a political emphasis.

• The major conflict in Finnish theatre at this time existed between people speaking "high Swedish" and those speaking "Finland-Swedish." A trend toward unification existed, but no real resolution was reached.

• In Denmark theatre languished and depended largely on foreign playwrights.

THE SOVIET UNION

• The post-Revolution Soviet Union under Josef Stalin determined to use theatre as part of its propaganda endeavor, and under the People's Commissariat for Education, Vsevolod Meyerhold (1874-1940) was appointed head of all theatre. Following his pre-Revolution concepts, first in the Theatre of the Revolution (1922-1924) and in his own Meyerhold Theatre (1923-1938), he promoted some exceptional theatre until, accused of "formalism," he was arrested and either was executed or died in prison. It was a difficult time for theatre, as the several regenerations of the Moscow Art Theatre, such as the Realistic Theatre, reveal. Possibly the work of both Theodore Kommissarzhevsky (1874-1954) and Alexander Tairov (1885-1950) showed Russian experimentation at its most effective.

• Realism was a familiar theatre term. Socialist Realism, which Maxim Gorky (1868-1936) promoted during the 1930's, was essentially Realism according to the Communist Party Line and the ideas of Vladimir Lenin and Karl Marx. Among Soviet playwrights of the 1930's, Nikolai Pogodin (1900-1962) and Alexander Afinogenov (1904-1941) would be designated "conformist" writers.

LATIN AMERICA

• A single characteristic of all theatre-minded Latin American countries is a fascination with theatre groups. Most countries established numerous theatre companies, most of them short-lived: Mexico's Teatro de Ulises and Teatro de Orientación; Argentina's Teatro de Pueblo (one of many with a Marxist bias); Brazil's Amateur Theatre of Permanbuco (1941) and Black Experimental Theatre (1944); Venezuela's Teatro Obrero (1938) and Venezuelan Company of Plays and Comedies (1939). Nicaraguan playwright Pablo Antonio Cuadra (b. 1912) wrote for El Teatro Lope in Grenada.

• Colombian playwright Luis Enrique Osorio (1896-1966) founded a journal to promote the drama, as well as a national theatre company, and wrote plays critical of Colombian manners and society.

THE UNITED STATES

• By the time World War I ended in 1918, the Little Theatre Movement was progressing vigorously, and American playwrights, actors and designers had organized. "New Stagecraft" techniques were filtered through the imagination of Robert Edmond Jones (1887-1959), who with Kenneth Macgowan (1888-1963) and Eugene O'Neill (1888-1953) formed a triumverate which helped bring success to the Provincetown Players.

• Although the Stock Market Crash helped to close the Provincetown, theatre companies continued to experiment. The economic conditions of the 1930's gave rise to a number of left-wing groups and playwrights, such as John Howard Lawson (1895-1977). The Group Theatre was organized by Lee Strasberg (1901-1982), Harold Clurman (1901-1980) and Cheryl Crawford (1902-1986).

• The Federal Theatre Project, sponsored by the Works Progress Administration, was headed by Hallie Flanagan Davis (1890-1969) and included the Living Newspaper productions and the Negro Theatre Unit. It ran into immediate censorship problems, however, before the government ended its sponsorship.

• Broadway plays of the period include *The Emperor Jones* (1920, O'Neill), *The Adding Machine* (1923, Rice), *What Price Glory?* (1924, Anderson and Laurence Stallings), *In Abraham's Bosom* (1926, Green), *Ah, Wilderness!* (1933, O'Neill), *Waiting for Lefty* (1935, Odets), *Dead End* (1935, Sidney Kingsley, b. 1906), *Mulatto* (1935, Hughes), *The Petrified Forest* (1935, Sherwood), *Our Town* (1938, Wilder), *The Little Foxes* (1939, Hellman), *The Man Who Came to Dinner* (1939, Kaufman and Moss Hart, 1904-1961), *Philadelphia Story* (1939, Philip Barry, 1896-1949), *The Time of Your Life* (1939, William Saroyan, 1908-1981), *There Shall Be No Night* (1940, Sherwood).

• The Playwrights' Company was formed by five authors -- Maxwell Anderson (1888-1959), Elmer Rice (1892-1967), Robert Sherwood (1896-1955), Sidney Howard (1891-1939) and S. N. Behrman (1893-1973) -- who were unhappy with the Theatre Guild.

World Theatre, 1916-1945

• This period was significant for advances in folk drama (*The Green Pastures,* 1930, by Marc Connelly, 1890-1880) and pageant drama (*The Lost Colony,* 1937, by Paul Green, 1894-1981), poetic drama by Maxwell Anderson (*Winterset,* 1935) and for a core of drama critics chosen especially for their skills in assessing theatre (Brooks Atkinson, 1894-1984, and John Mason Brown, 1900-1969).

• With the production of *Oklahoma!* (1943) by Richard Rodgers (1902-1970) and Oscar Hammerstein II (1895-1960), modern musical comedy began.

CANADA

• Canada's first serious playwright, Merill Denison (1893-1975), learned his art at the Hart House Theatre. Such plays as *The Weather Breeder* (1924) and *The Prize Winner* (1928) show his attitudes toward rural Canada.

• The period of Canadian theatre through 1945 is frequently referred to as "the touring era." Outside the larger cities theatre was either nonexistent or being slowly created by amateur groups, which were helped greatly by the Dominion Drama Festival in 1932. For French-speaking Canadians, theatres existed in Montreal and in the Catholic university structure.

AUSTRALIA

• After World War I, theatre management changed in Australia as it did in England from the actor-manager to the commercial entrepreneur. Variety theatre and touring stars fulfilled the needs of most managements, who also relied on foreign plays. Little theatres provided outlets for the work of Australian playwrights, such as Oriel Gray and Sydney Tomholt.

World Theatre after 1945

THE MIDDLE EAST

1946
    1948 Republic of Israel established
    Little theatre movement in Turkey
    1952 The Little Stage established by
        Mushin Ertugrel in Turkey
    1953 Telem, Israeli effort to bring
        theatre to immigrants
    1954 Municipal Theatre of Tunis opens
    Turkish playwrights: Haldun Taner
        (b. 1915), Aziz Nesin (b. 1915)

    1958 Israeli National Theatre begins
    National Art Group in Iran; Shakin
        Sarkissian (1912-1966), founder
    Tawfiq Al-Hakim (1898-1987),
        Egyptian playwright
1960
    1961 National Theatre founded in Syria
    Haifa Municipal Theatre and School
        of Stage Arts

    1964 Office of Dramatic Arts opened
        in Iranian Ministry of Culture
    Growth of little theatre in Turkey
    1967 1st permanent regional company
        in Kef, Tunisia
    1967 *Ta'zieh* 1st presented at
        Festival of Arts in Shiraz, Iran
    1967 Israeli Six-Day War
    1969 Performance Workshop opens
        in Teheran
1970   Gholain Hosein Saede (b. 1935),
        Iranian playwright
    1976 *Ta'zieh* at Festival of Arts
    Mid 1970's 6 municipal and 20
        private theatres in Istanbul
    1978-1979 Iranian Revolution
    1981 *The Passion of Job* by Hanock
        Levin (1943-), Israeli playwright

AFRICA

1947 National Theatre Organization
    established in South Africa
c. 1948 Nairobi African Dramatic
    Society founded

1957 Independence of Ghana
1958-1961 Experimental theatre
    established in Ghana by Efua T.
    Sutherland (1924-)

1960 Independence of Nigeria, Mali
    and Cameroon
1960 Wole Soyinka (1934-) founds
    Masks group in Nigeria
1962 Duro Ladipo (1931-1978) founds
    traveling theatre in Nigeria
1963 Independence of Kenya
1965 Makerere Free Traveling
    Theatre established in East Africa
Playwrights: Ama Ato Aidoo (1942- ,
    Ghana), G. Ozónô-Mbia (1939- ,
    Cameroon), Ngugi wa Thiong'o
    1938- , Kenya), Yulisa Maddy
    (1936- , Sierra Leone), Lewis Nkosi
    (1936- South Africa), Alfred
    Hutchinson (1924- , South Africa)
1970's -1980's Black political town-
    ship theatres in South Africa
Athol Fugard (1932-), South African
    playwright
1980's Appearance of Black Trade Union
    Workers' Theatre units
1982 Pec Repertory Theatre in Lagos;
    John Pepper Clark (1936-) founder

World Theatre after 1945

INDIA AND SOUTHEAST ASIA

1946 1944-1960 Prithvi Theatre popular
in North India
1947 Partition and independence of
India and Pakistan
1948 Mahatma Ghandi assassinated
1949 Siam becomes Thailand
1949 Indonesian independence

1954 National Academy of Music, Dance
and Drama opens in New Delhi
1954 1st National Drama Festival in India
1955 Indonesian National Theatre
Academy founded
Late 1950's Prime Minister U Nu of
Burma writes *The People Win
Through*
1959 National School of Drama opens
in New Delhi
1960 *Sendratasi,* new dance-drama in
Indonesia
1960 Kalidasa Festival in Ujjain, India

1963 Malaysia established

1967 Philippine Educational Theatre
Association founded

1969 People's Little Theatre opens in
Calcutta
1970 Only 2 English-speaking theatres in
India: Madras Players and the
Theatre Group in Bombay
1973 Protest theatre in Philippines
1980's Many amateur theatres in India
Indian playwrights: Mohan Rakesh
(1925-1973), Badal Sircar (1925-),
Asif Currimbhoy (1925?-)

PEOPLE'S REPUBLIC OF CHINA

1946 Opera version of *The White-
haired Girl*

1949 The Communist Take-over

1957 The "100 Flowers Campaign"
1957 50th anniversary of production
of *Uncle Tom's Cabin,* in Beijing

1958-1960 The Big Leap Forward

1961 Mei Lan-fang, actor, dies

1964-1968 Cultural Revolution
1966 Chiang Ching selects 5 Model
Revolutionary Peking Operas
Playwrights: Ts'ao Yu (1910-),
Lao Sheh (1897-1966), Tien Han
(1898-1968), Kuo Mo-jo (1892-
1978), Hung Shen (1893-1955),
Hsiung Fo-hsi (1900-1965)

1976 Mao Tse-tung dies
1980 Ts'ao Yu tours United States
1983 *Fifteen Cases of Divorce* by
Liu Hsu-kang
1984   3,397 theatre troupes in China

World Theatre after 1945

1946　1947 Theatre Arts Association
　　　　organized in Korea
　　　　1948 Korea divided (North and
　　　　South)

1950 South Korea establishes
　National Theatre
1950-1953 Korean War

Kinoshita Junji (1914-), Japanese
　shingeki playwright

1960　After 1960 Post-*shingeki* move-
　　　　ment toward "dramaturgy
　　　　of metamorphosis"
　　　　1962 South Korean Research Institute
　　　　for Dramatic Art established

Japanese playwrights: Kobo Abe
　(1924-), Mishima Yukio (1925-
　1970), Fukuda Yoshiyuki (1931-),
　Akimoto Matsuyo (1911-)

1970　1970's North Korean theatre used
　　　　as propaganda for Kim Il-Song
　　　　1970's Innovative Japanese theatre
　　　　troupes: Suzuki Tadashi (1939-),
　　　　experimentor; Black Tent Theatre
　　　　of Satoh Makoto; Situation
　　　　Theatre of Kara Juro

ITALY AND SPAIN

1947 Creation of *teatro stabile* in Italy
1947 Piccolo Teatro, touring theatre,
　Milan

1950 Teatro de Agitacion Social formed
　by Alfonso Sastre (1926-), Spanish
　playwright

1960　10 residential theatre troupes
　active in Italy
Italian playwrights: Ugo Betti
　(1892-1953), Diego Fabbri (1911-
　1980)
Franco Zeffirelli (1923-), Italian
　director
Spanish playwrights: Antonio Buero
　Vallejo (1916-), Alfonso Paso
　(1926-1977), Fernando Arrabal
　(1932-)

Late 1960's New Spanish Theatre
　avant garde movement
1970 La Comune founded by Dario Fo
　(1926-), Italian playwright
1974 National Festival of Youth
　Theatre in Italy
1975 Death of Franco
1977 Democracy restored to Spain
National Dramatic Center in Spain

World Theatre after 1945

FRANCE AND WESTERN EUROPE

1946 1947 Subsidized "small dramatic centers" established in France

French playwrights: Jean Anouilh (1910-1987), Henri de Montherlant (1896-1972), Jean Paul Sartre (1905-1980), Albert Camus (1913-1960), Samuel Beckett (1906-1989), Eugene Ionesco (1912-1990), Jean Genet (1910-1986), Arthur Adamov (1908-1971)

French actor-directors: Jean-Louis Barrault (b. 1910), Jean Vilar (1912-1971)

1960 1962 Decentralizing French theatre: government subsidy of new cultural centers

1964 Théâtre du Soliel founded by Ariane Mnouchkine (1934-)

French actor-directors: Antoine Vilez (1930-), Roger Blin (1907-1984)

Swiss playwrights: Max Frisch (1911-1991), Friedrich Dürrenmatt (1921-1990)

Swiss Theatres: Théâtre Populaire Romand (1961), Das Theater Für Den Kanton Zurich (1971)

Late 1960's Internationale Nieuwe Scene established in Belgium

Late 1960's Akatie Tomaat, Dutch campaign against traditional drama

1970 1970's New Dutch theatres: Appel (1972), Onafhankelijk Toneel (1974)

1972 Théâtre de l'Espérance founded in France by Jean-Pierre Vincent (1942-)

1975 Festival of Fools, Dutch fringe theatre, established

1980's New forms of theatre in Belguim

ENGLAND AND IRELAND

1946 75% of English theatres controlled by "The Group"

English playwrights: Terence Rattigan (1911-1977), Christopher Fry (b. 1907)

1951 Lyric Theatre founded in Belfast
1952 Agatha Christie's *The Mousetrap* opens at Ambassador Theatre, London

1956 English Stage Company founded
1957 Dublin Theatre Festival begins
English playwrights: John Osborne (1929-), Arnold Wesker (1932-), Peter Shaffer (1926-)
Irish Playwrights: Brendan Behan (1923-1964), Brian Friel (1929-), Thomas Kilroy (1934)
1961 Royal Shakespeare (Company) Theatre renamed
1963 Old Vic dissolved; National Theatre established
English playwrights: Harold Pinter (1930-), Joe Orton (1933-1967), David Storey (1933-), Tom Stoppard (1937-)
English directors: Peter Brook (1925-), Joan Littlewood (b. 1914), Peter Hall (1930-)
English actors: John Gielgud (1904-), Lawrence Olivier (1907-1989), Edith Evans (1888-1976), Michael Redgrave (1908-1985), Flora Robson (1902-1984), Peggy Ashcroft (1907-1991), Ralph Richardson (1902-1983)
1970's Growth of alternative theatres

1980's Declining interest in experimentation

GERMANY AND EASTERN EUROPE

1946   1947 Komische Oper founded in East Berlin
1947 Bertolt Brecht (1898-1956) returns to
Europe
1948-1949 All Rumanian and Hungarian
theatres nationalized
1948-1968 Czechoslovakian theatre follows
Marxist thought
1949 Polish Writer's Union declares Social
Realism "the true art form"
1949 Berliner Ensemble founded in East Berlin
Strong growth of West German theatre
1951 Erwin Piscator (1893-1966) returns to
Germany
1951 Bayreuth Festival revived

Czech experimental theatre: Josef Svoboda
(1920-), designer; Balustrade Theatre
(1958), the Actors' Club (1965)
1960   Gunter Grass (1927-), German playwright
Slawomir Mrözek (1930-), Polish
playwright
Czech playwrights: Václav Havel (1936-),
Pavel Kohout (1928-)
Polish directors: Ida Kaminska (1899-
1970), Jerzy Grotowski (1933-)
Hungarian playwrights: Istrán Örkeny
(1912-1979), Andras Sütö (1927-)
1960's German "theater of fact": Rolf
Hochhuth (1931-), Peter Weiss (1916-)
German playwrights: Feter Handke
(1942-), Franz Kroetz (1946-)

1968 Soviets invade Czechoslovakia and
purge theatres
1970   1970's Brechtian tradition accepted
in Germany
1979-1981 Triumph of Solidarity in Poland
Mid 1980's Polish theatre fights restrictions
Late 1980's Communist Bloc dissolves;
Berlin Wall comes down; unrest in
Eastern Europe

SCANDINAVIA

1945-1950 Studio Theatre opens
in Norway
Renaissance in Finnish theatre
Finnish playwrights: Paavo
Haavikko (1931-), Inkeré
Kilpiners (1926-),Viejo Meri
(1928-)

1962 Fidteatret opens in Denmark
1960's-1970's New State Theatre
Schools in Stockholm,
Gothernburg and Malmö
1960's Growing political consciousness in Danish theatre
Proliferation of Swedish theatres:
Fickteatern (1966), Theatre 9
(1969), Skånska Teater (1973),
Earth Circus (1977)
Swedish playwrights: Kent
Andersson (1933-), Per Enquist
(1934-), Suzanne Osten (1944-)
1960-1970's "Happenings" in
Denmark; *Santa Claus Army*
1970's New subsidized regional
theatres in Norway: Tromsø
(1971), Skien (1975), Forde
(1977), Mo i Rana (1979)
Norwegian playwrights: Tormod
Skagestad (1920-), Johan Borgen
(1902-1977), Jens Björneboe (1920-
1977), Klaus Hagerup (1942-)

World Theatre after 1945

THE SOVIET UNION

1946

1949 Party control of theatre
    tightened
1950's Style of Social Realism
    maintained
1950's Plays used largely as
    propaganda "for social
    betterment"
1953 Joseph Stalin dies
1957 The Contemporary Theatre,
    1st new theatre since 1930's,
    founded

Late 1950's Loosening of bonds in
    post-Stalin era

1960

1964 Moscow Theatre of Drama
    and Comedy founded by Yuri
    Lyubimov (1917-), director and
    playwright

1970   Issue plays by Aleksandr Gelman:
    The Party Committee Meeting
    (1975), *Feedback Circuit* (1977)

Playwrights: Aleksandr Vampilov
    (1937-1972), Aleksei Nikolaevich
    Arbuzo (b. 1908), Edvard
    Stanislavovich Radvinsky (1938-)

LATIN AMERICA

"Generation of 1950" in Chile
1953 Teatro Experimental Universitario
    established in Quito
1953 Club de Teatro established in Lima;
    Sebastian Bondy (1924-1965), founder
1950's Teatro Experimental de Cali of
    Enrique Buenaventura (1928-),
    Colombia
Samuel Eichelbaum (1894-1967),
    Argentinian playwright

New theatres established in Rio
    de Janeiro: Arena, Workshop,
    Opinion Theatre
1960's Latin American Theatre Research
    Center opens in Caracas
Augusto Boal (1931-), Brazilian
    playwright and director

1960's Andres Morris (1928-) founds
    Teatro Nacional, Honduras
1969 Colombian Theatre Corpora-
    tion unites 100+ theatres
1969 Taller de Experimentacion
    Teatral opens in Chile

1970 Decline of Theatre in Brazil
1973 Free Center of Theatre Arts
    opens in Mexico
1973 Coup and repression in Chile
Playwrights: Griselda Gambaro
    1928- , Argentina), Carlos
    Fuentes (1929- , Mexico), Raul
    Ruiz (1943- , Chile)

World Theatre after 1945

THE CARIBBEAN

1946 The Whitehall Players founded
in Trinidad

1950 St. Lucia Arts Council founded

1957 Theatre Guild of Guyana
founded
1959 Trinidad Theatre Workshop
founded
1959 Revolution in Cuba; National
Theatre School opens
1960 Cuban playwrights: Virgilio
Piñera (1912-1979), Carlos Felipe
(1914-1975), Anton Arrufat (1935-),
José Triana (1932-), Nickolas
Dorr (1947-)
1962 National School of Art opens
in Cuba
1960's Jamaica's National Drama
School founded
1960's Little Carib Theatre opens in
Trinidad
1964 *The Tragedy of King Christophe*
by Aimé Césaire (1913-), Martinique
1967 *Dream on Monkey Mountain* by
Derek Walcott (1930-), St. Lucia
1968 Teatro Escanbray opens in Cuba
1970 Trinidadian playwrights: Errol
Hill (1921-), Jack Archibald
Jamaican playwrights: Barry Reckord,
Cicely Waite-Smith, Samuel Hillary
Guyanese playwrights: Frank Pilgrim,
Sheik Sadech
1980's Wide use of theatre in Cuba;
government support and censorship

THE UNITED STATES

1946-1947 American Repertory Company
1946-1965 Period of great American
musical comedies
1947 Actors Studio opens
1948 Living Theatre, founded by Judith
Malina (1926-) and Julian Beck
(1925-1985)
1949-1950 Only 59 new plays during
Broadway season
1953 Phoenix Theatre founded by Norris
Houghton (1909-) and T. Edward
Hambleton (1911-)
1954 New York Shakespeare Festival
founded by Joseph Papp (1921-1991)
Playwrights: Tennessee Williams
(1911-1983), William Inge (1913-
1973), Arthur Miller (1915-),
Lorraine Hansberry (1930-1965)
1960 Association of Producing Artists
founded
Off off Broadway groups: Café Cino
(1958), La Mama (1962), Open
Theatre (1963), The Performance
Group (1967)
Playwrights: Neil Simon (1927-),
Edward Albee (1928-)
Regional theatres: Arena Stage,
Washington (1950), Guthrie Theatre,
Minneapolis (1963), Actors Theatre
of Louisville (1964)
1968 Ontological Hysteric Theatre;
Richard Foreman (1937-), founder
Black theatre companies: Black Arts
Rep (1964), Negro Ensemble (1968)
1972 Off Off Broadway Alliance links
theatre companies
1973 *A Chorus Line,* longest running
show on Broadway
Playwrights: Amiri Baraka (1934-),
Lanford Wilson (1937-), Sam
Shepard (1943-), August Wilson
(1945-), Beth Henley (1952-)

World Theatre after 1945

CANADA	AUSTRALIA

1946

1951 Le Théâtre de Nouveau Monde opens in Montreal

1957 Canada Council formed; state support for theatre and artists

1958 National Institute of Dramatic Art established

1960   National Theatre School founded

French-Canadian playwrights: Paul Toupin (1918-), Marcel Dubé (1930-), Francois Moreau (1941-), Michel Tremblay (1942-)

1960's-1970's Popularity of musical satires

1968-1973 Regional theatres organized in Winnipeg, Vancouver, Edmonton, Regina, Montreal, Fredericton, Toronto, Sudbury, London and Thunder Bay

c. 1969 Movement in Toronto toward off off Broadway type companies

1970   Alternative theatre movement
Festival of Underground Theatre held in Toronto
1972 Toronto Free Theatre opens
Playwrights: George F. Walker (1947-), David French (1939-), Carol Bolt (1941-)
1976 Parti Québécois government

1967-1975 Alternative theatre
1968 State supported theatres open in all state capitals
Regional theatre companies supported in Adelaide (1965), Brisbane (1969), Hobart, (1973)

Playwrights: Patrick White (1912-), David Williamson (1942-), Alexander Buzo (1944-), Stephen Sewell (1953-), Louis Nowra (1950-)
1975 Growth in youth, women's and Aboriginal theatre

THE MIDDLE EAST

• Immediately following World War II, theatre was encouraged in Turkey and in Iran, which first accepted professional Western style drama at this time. Israelis used the theatre more expediently in their settlements. Egypt's theatre was well defined, while among the countries of North Africa, only Tunisia had made a conserted effort to establish a theatre tradition.

• Among all Middle Eastern countries, only Egypt contributed a major dramatist -- Tawfiq Al-Hakim (1898-1987), who after 1950 wrote plays of social criticism such as *The Sultan's Dilemma* (1960) and the absurdist play, *The Tree Climber* (1962). Other Egyptian playwrights included Rashad Rushdy, with *A Journey Outside the Wall*, and Yusef Idris, with *Farfoors*.

• Gholain Hosein Saede (b. 1935), an Iranian playwright, gained a reputation with such plays as *Woe to the Vanquished* (1971).

• In Israel, A. B. Yehoshua's *A Night in May* (1968) reflected on the Six Day War, while his *Soul of a Jew* (1982) searched social consciousness. Hanock Levin's (1943-), satirical play, *The Passion of Job* (1981), may best represent modern Israeli drama.

AFRICA

• Numerous Sub-Saharan countries gained their independence from colonial powers about 1960. With these governmental changes came varied and substantial interest in theatre -- sometimes a remnant remaining from the colonizing power, sometimes initiated by a person who had been educated abroad, sometimes by Africans interested in sustaining native theatre or fusing aspects of it with elements of Western drama.

• After the 1960's there was substantial work by playwrights from several African countries. Nigerian theatre received the greatest international attention, primarily through the efforts of Wole Soyinka (1934-), Nobel Prize winner in 1986 for such plays as *A Dance of the Forests* (1960), *The Strong Breed* (1963). Both John Pepper Clark (1935-), with *The Song of A Goat* (1962), and Duro Ladipo (1931-1978), with his traveling theatre and his work with Yoruba opera, also made distinctive contributions. A relationship with universities, particularly those at Ibadan and Ifé, enhanced theatre in Nigeria.

• Like many other African playwrights, and Third World playwrights in general, Efua T. Sutherland (1924-) established an experimental theatre (1958-1961) which enhanced his later works, such as *Edufa* (1967). Another Guyanese playwright, Ama Ato Aidoo (1942-), wrote *The Dilemma of a Ghost* (1964) and *Anowa* (1970). In Cameroon G. Oyónô-Mbia (1939-) showed French influence in *Three Suitors, One Husband* (1964), while Victor Elearne Musinga, with his own theatre group, revealed an English background in *The Trials of Ngowo* (1973). Kenya's major playwright, Ngugi wa Thiong'o (1938-), wrote *This Time Tomorrow* (1968). Yulisa Amadu Maddy (1936-), Sierra Leone, founded the Gbakanda Afrikan Tiata and wrote *Obasai* and *Gbana Bendu,* both published in 1971.

• Athol Fugard (1932-), the major South African playwright, wrote *The Blood Knot* (1961) and *Sizwe Bansi Is Dead* (1972). Among other South African playwrights are Lewis Nkosi (1936-) and Alfred Hutchinson (1924-).

• Among the touring theatres in Africa were Duro Ladipo's personal theatre, whose tours were recorded on film, and the Makerere Free Traveling Theatre (1965-) in East Africa. By offering everything from local plays to versions of Shakespeare in English, Swahili and local dialects, the Makerere Theatre brought entertainment to a wide area.

INDIA AND SOUTHEAST ASIA

• After 1947 there was a cultural resurgence in India which revived interest in traditional and folk theatres. State supported organizations were created for research, performance training and production. The First National Drama Festival in 1954 produced a Sanskrit play, as later festivals would also do. At the same time there was spontaneous interest in Western stage techniques which would be presented in historical plays, romantic plays and the social realistic plays of protest and issues.

• With relatively few commercial theatres in India, the amateur companies provided the theatre's life blood. Calcutta boasted 3,000 registered amateur groups, Bombay 500 and Delhi several dozen. Among the better known groups were Calcutta's Bohorupu, Bombay's Goa Hindu Association's Theatre Wing and the Indian National Theatre.

• The size of India and the different languages spoken presented undeniable difficulties for the playwrights who sought a national reputation. Mohan Rakesh (1925-1973) wrote in Hindi, Girish Karnad (1938-) in Kannada, Badal Sircar (1925-) in Bengali and Asif Currimbhoy (1925?-) in English. Rajinder Paul, a playwright of New Delhi, edited a journal entitled *ENACT,* translating plays into English.

• With independence from colonial powers, new Southeast Asian countries generally provided state support for the renewal of traditional theatre arts. In many instances, Western style theatre was not considered of primary importance. In Thailand, *lakon phut,* or spoken drama, remained largely of interest to the intelligencia. Burma (Myanmar after 1989) maintained a traditional approach to its theatre. Malaysia, with its strong ties to the United States, both reaffirmed its concern for tradtional theatre arts and imitated the West in the works of such playwrights as Amany Had Salleh, Mustafa Kamil Yassin and Nooridin Hassan. The influence of Western drama was strong in the Philippines.

CHINA

• *The White-haired Girl,* the most significant theatrical production of the People's Republic of China, started as a Yangko folk opera in 1944. Based on an event during Mao's Long March (1934-1935), the work was revised in opera form, made into a film in 1950, a ballet in 1955, a Peking Opera in 1958 and a color film in 1972.

• From 1949 to 1976 theatre was made to serve Mao's teaching. As political theories changed during the "Hundred Flowers Campaign" and the "Big Leap Forward," so did the kind of plays being written. During the Cultural Revolution, Chiang Ching, Mao's wife and an actress, endorsed the Five Model Revolutionary Peking Operas: *The Red Lantern, Raid on the White Tiger Regiment, Taking the Bandits' Stronghold, Shachiapang* and *On the Docks.*

• Control of the theatre "as a weapon" was thorough, although "bootleg" performances of traditional Chinese operas probably took place. After Mao's death in 1976, more revolutionary operas and plays were written, and themes changed as policy demanded, as seen in *Fifteen Cases of Divorce* (1984) by Liu Hsu-kang, a topic quite foreign to Mao's Puritan philosophy.

JAPAN

• Experimentation took place in the Japanese theatre, both in traditional forms and in the newly introduced Western drama. Kobo Abe (1924-) followed the absurdist tradition in *The Man Who Turned into a Stick* (1957) and *Friends* (1967). Mishima Yukio (1925-1970) created several modern *noh* plays.

• After 1960 a concern for the past influenced the Japanese to create a "dramaturgy of metamorphosis" in which the gods once more appeared on the stage. *Find Hokamadari!* (1964) by Fukuda Yoshizuki (1931-) was an early play to employ the technique, as did *Kaison, the Priest of Hitachi* (1965) by Akinoto Matsuyo (1911-).

ITALY AND SPAIN

• Italy's creation of *teatro stabile* was an attempt to establish permanent companies comparable in quality to the popular touring companies. These permanent companies included Teatro d'Arte of Genoa (1951) and Teatro Stabile of Turin (1955).

• Italian playwriting of the period was generally undistinguished. Ugo Betti's (1892-1953) *Crime on Goat Island* (1946) and the Catholic orientation of Diego Fabbri (1911-1980) in *Christian Ambiguity* (1954) represented early efforts. Dario Fo (1926-) had more international impact with biting commentary on current events in such plays as *Accidental Death of an Anarchist* (1970).

World Theatre after 1945

• After the death of Franco in 1975, Spanish theatre became more vibrant, although Alfonso Sastre (1926-) had already made a strong impression as both playwright and theorist with *Drama and Society* (1956) and *Revolution and Criticism of Culture* (1970). Several plays such as *Death Squad* (1953) distinguished his work. Fernando Arrabal (1932-), who left Spain in the 1950's, made his contribution to avant garde theatre in France with *The Automobile Graveyard* (1967) and later psychological shockers described as Panic Theatre.

FRANCE

• For a generation after World War II, French audiences found excitement in the work of innovative actor-directors and a variety of new existentialist and absurdist playwrights (so dubbed by Martin Esslin in *The Theatre of the Absurd,* 1961). Existentialists included Jean Paul Sartre (1905-1980) with *The Flies* (1943) and *The Condemned of Altona* (1959) and Albert Camus (1913-1960) with *Caligula* (1945). Absurdist playwrights included Samuel Beckett (1906-1989) with *Waiting for Godot* (1953) and *Endgame* (1957), Eugène Ionesco (1912-1990) with *The Chairs* (1952) and *Rhinoceros* (1960), Jean Genet (1910-1986) with *The Maids* (1947) and Arthur Adamov (1908-1971) with *Ping Pong* (1955).

• Dissatisfaction in theatre circles appeared in the 1960's. Afterwards, French directors were more inspired than French playwrights.

ENGLAND AND IRELAND

• The efforts of Prince Littler, through The Group, to control English theatre cast its shadow. Vitality, however, appeared with the English Stage Company in 1956 and the innovations of the Theatre Workshop (founded in 1945) under the direction of Joan Littlewood (b. 1914) until her resignation in 1961. With the decline of the Old Vic, the National Theatre got its beginning in 1963 in the Old Vic building, with the National Theatre complex completed in 1977. The English Stage Company, the Royal Shakespeare and the National Theatre Company became the three major companies in England .

• Plays by British dramatists included *The Browning Version* (1949) by Terence Rattigan (1911-1977), *Look Back in Anger* (1956) by John Osborne(1929-), *The Royal Hunt of the Sun* (1964) by Peter Shaffer (1926-), *The Old Ones* (1972) by Arnold Wesker (1932-), *The Birthday Party* (1958), by Harold Pinter (1930-), *Loot* (1966) by Joe Orton (1933-1967), *The Changing Room* (1971) by David Storey (1933-), *Travesties* (1974) by Tom Stoppard (1937-), *The Knack* (1961) by Ann Jellicoe (1927-), *How the Other Half Loves* (1970) by Alan Ayckbourn (1939-) and *Educating Rita* (1979) by Willy Russell (1947-).

• Irish plays included *The Hostage* (1958) by Brendan Behan (1923-1964) and *Philadelphia, Here I Come!* (1964) by Brian Friel (1929-).

GERMANY AND EASTERN EUROPE

• Important German plays of the period included *The Wicked Cooks* (1961) by Günter Grass (1927-) and *Marat/Sade* (1964) by Peter Weiss. (1916-) *Tango* (1964) by Slawomir Mrözek (1930-) represents Polish drama.

SCANDINAVIA

• None of the Scandinavian countries could produce a distinguished dramatist after World War II. There was, however, theatrical activity, mainly in Norway and Sweden. Both Finland and Denmark emphasized theatre as socially or politically useful.

THE SOVIET UNION

• After a long decade of straight-forward proganda theatre, the Soviet Union allowed modified freedom to playwrights after Stalin's death and provided some support for theatre. The concept of Social Realism disappeared slowly, although playwrights of the 1970's used comedy effectively to explore the national and social conscience.

LATIN AMERICA

• Theatre in Latin America had an uneven passage as winds from Europe and the United States created enthusiasm while political intrigues undermined both professional and amateur efforts. National theatre festivals, however, assisted theatre artists in their work.

• Among South American playwrights were Andrés Lizarraga (1919-1982, Argentina), Osvaldo Dragun (1929- , Argentina), Luis Heiremans (1928-1964, Chile), Sergio Vodanovic (1926- , Chile), Alonzo Alegria (1940- , Peru), Enrique Buenaventura (1928- , Colombia), Fernando González Cajiao (1938- , Colombia), Demtrio Ajuilera Malta (1907-1979, Ecuador).

• Mexican playwrights included Emelio Carballido (1925-), Sergio Magaña (1924-) and Jenés Gonzalez Dávila (1942).

• Among Central American countries, Honduras has promoted theatre through Teatro Nacional and Teatro la Fragua in Progreso (1979). Costa Rica established the Grupo Tierra Negra (1973) and a journal, *Escena* (1979), for drama criticism. Playwrights included Daniel Gallegos (1930- , Costa Rica), Rolando Steiner (1935- , Nicaragua) and José de Jesús Martinez (1928- , Panama).

World Theatre after 1945

THE UNITED STATES

• Until the 1980's the United States produced the best musical plays in the world. An era starting with *Oklahoma!* in 1943 saw such successes as *Carousel* (1945), *South Pacific* (1949) and *The King and I* (1952) by Rodgers and Hammerstein; *Guys and Dolls* (1950) by Frank Loesser (1910-1969); *My Fair Lady* (1956) by Alan J. Lerner (1918-1986) and Frederik Loewe (1804-1988); *West Side Story* (1957) by Leonard Bernstein (1918-1990), Arthur Laurants (1918-) and Stephen Sondheim (1930-); *Gypsy* (1959) by Laurants and Sondheim and *Fiddler on the Roof* (1964) by Jerry Bock (1925-) and Sheldon Harnick (1924-).

• The two greatest playwrights of the mid 20th century were Tennessee Williams (1911-1983) and Arthur Miller (1915-). Miller will be remembered for a number of plays -- *All My Sons* (1947), *Death of a Salesman* (1949), *The Crucible* (1953), *A View from the Bridge* (1955), *After the Fall* (1964), *Incident at Vichy* (1964) and *The Prize* (1968) -- plus a number of essays contributing to American dramatic theory. Williams is remembered for *The Glass Menagerie* (1945), *A Streetcar Named Desire* (1947), *Summer and Smoke* (1948), *Cat on a Hot Tin Roof* (1955), *Sweet Bird of Youth* (1959) and *The Night of the Iguana* (1961).

• After 1960 several playwrights wrote a sufficient number of successful plays to warrant consideration, among them Edward Albee with *Who's Afraid of Virginia Woolf?* (1962) and *Tiny Alice* (1964); Neil Simon with *The Odd Couple* (1965) and *Brighton Beach Memoirs* (1983); and Sam Shepard (1943-) with *Tooth of the Crime* (1972) and *Buried Child* (1978).

• After World War II, spiraling costs of Broadway productions stimulated the formation of numerous regional and non-professional theatre companies in every state. By the late 1960's theatres devoted to black, feminist and gay issues had appeared. Interest in children's theatre and youth theatre grew. Avant garde playwrights and theorists convened at the Wooster Group or Mabou Mines in New York or such theatres as the Omaha Magic Theatre.

CANADA AND AUSTRALIA

• Theatre in both countries took steps in similar directions. First, there was government money to support central and regional theatres and theatre artists. Soon, alternative theatres appeared in each country as playwrights experimented and, as the 1980's approached, money was less freely given. In Canada, however, two distinct theatre trends were developing: English-language theatre and French-language theatre.

The Greek Theatre

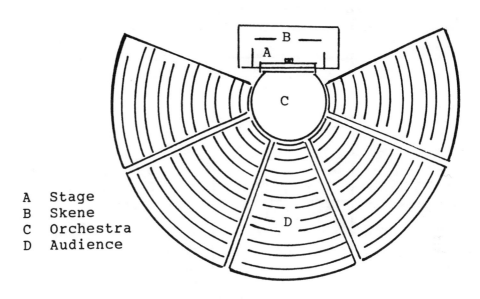

A Stage
B Skene
C Orchestra
D Audience

The Roman Theatre

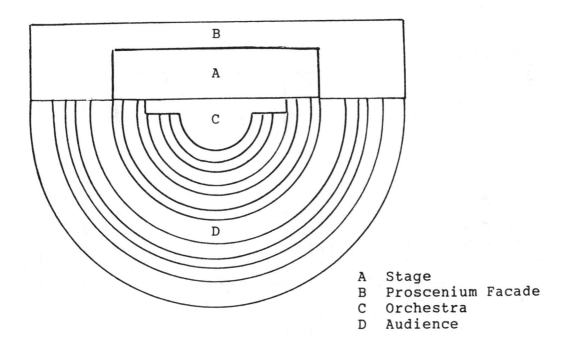

A Stage
B Proscenium Facade
C Orchestra
D Audience

The Sanskrit Theatre
(as described in the <u>Natyasastra</u>)

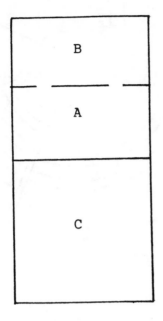

A Stage
B Resting Area
C Audience

The Chinese Theatre

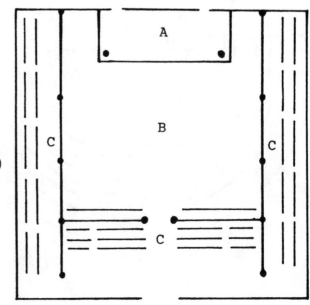

A Stage
B Fish Pond
    (tables and stools)
C Raised Seats

The <u>Noh</u> Theatre

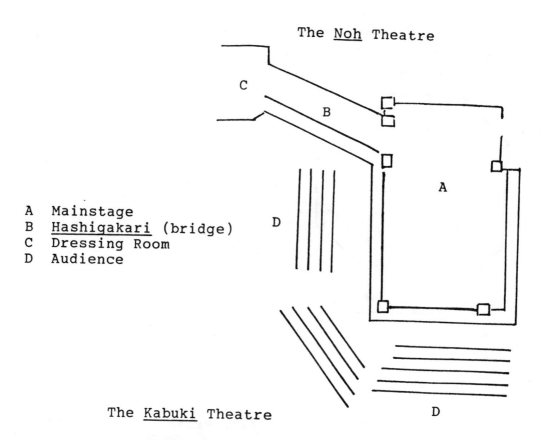

A   Mainstage
B   <u>Hashigakari</u> (bridge)
C   Dressing Room
D   Audience

The <u>Kabuki</u> Theatre

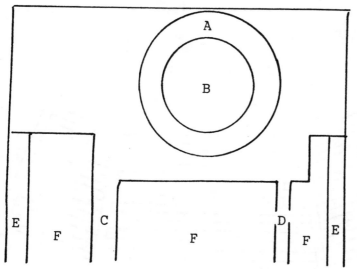

A   Revolving Stage
B   Revolving Inner
     Stage
C   <u>Hanamichi</u>
     (flower path)
D   Temporary
     <u>Hanamichi</u>
E   Boxes
F   Audience

The Elizabethan Theatre
(public outdoor)

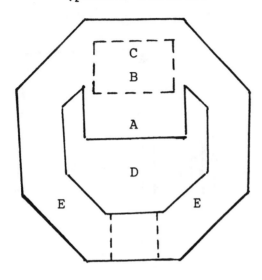

A Forestage
B Canopy
C Balcony
D Standing Room (open air)
E Galleries (on 3 levels)

The Contemporary Proscenium Theatre

A Stage
B Proscenium Arch
C Apron
D Audience

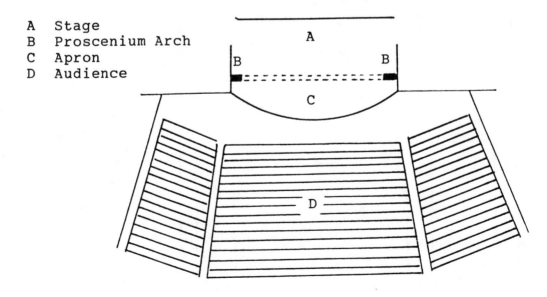

Index

M

Mabou Mines 118
Macedo, Joaquim Manuel de 82
Macgowan, Kenneth 103
Machiavelli, Niccolo 44
Mackaye, Steele 83, 89
Macready, William 66, 74, 76
Macropedius, Georgius 46
Madách, Imre 81
Maddy, Yulisa 105, 114
Madras Players 106
Madrid, José Fernandez 68
Madwoman of Chaillot, The 101
Maeterlinck, Maurice 81, 87, 100
Magyar Elektra 46
Mahabhasya 17, 20
Mahendravekramarasman 27
Maids, The 116
Makerere Free Traveling Theatre 105,
    114
Makyong 85
Malina, Judith 111
Malta, Demtrio Ajuilera 117
Man Who Came to Dinner, The 103
Man Who Turned into a Stick, The 115
Man Without a Soul 102
Magaña, Sergio 117
Mandragola 44
Manohra 78
Manora 78, 85
*Manual for Constructing Theatrical
    Scene Machines* 44
Marat/Sade 117
Margaret Fleming 83, 90
Maria Hoedeken 46
Maria Magdalena 75
Marivaux, Pierre 56, 61
Marlowe, Christopher 46, 51
Marriage of Figaro, The 73
Marriage of Sita, The 77
Marston, John 51
Marti, José 82
Martinez, José de Jesús 117
Mask and the Face, The 100
Masquerade 75

Massinger, Philip 51
Mathews, Cornelius 69
Maugham, Somerset 94, 101
Mauro, Gaspare 60
Mayakovsky, Vladimir 95
Mazoni, Alessandro 65
Meddah 32, 35, 42, 53, 63
Medea (Greece) 16
Medea (Rome) 24
Mei Lan-fang 106
Meiningen Players 81, 78, 88
Memphite Drama 8, 10
Menaechmi 21
Menander 14, 16
Men's Kabuki 50, 54
Menschenhaus und Reue 74
Mercury Theatre (London) 84
Meri, Viejo 109
Messenius, Johannes 46, 52
Metamora 69, 76
*Metamora; or The Last of the
    Polywogs* 76
Metastasio, Pietro 55, 60
Meyerhold, Vsevelod 82, 88, 95, 102
Michelena, Leopoldo Ayala 82
Middle Comedy 14, 16
Middleton, Thomas 51
Military Counselor, The 30
Miller, Arthur 111, 118
Ming Huang, Emperor 28, 30, 58
Minna von Barnhelm 74
Minturno, Antonio 50
Misanthrope, The 61
Miser, The 61
Miser, The (Egypt) 70
Mishima, Yukio 107, 115
Miss Julie 88
Miss Sara Sampson 74
Mitchell, William 76
Mnouchkine, Ariane 108
Mo i Rani 109
Moberg, Wilhelm 95
*Modern Theatre: Points of View
    and Attack* 95, 102
Molière 56, 60, 61, 70
Molina, Tirso de 51

Le théâtre est toujours la secrétion d'une civilisation;
la société, dans sa forme actuelle, a le théâtre qu'elle
mérite.

Louis Jouvet

The Authors

Walter J. Meserve holds the rank of Distinguished Professor in the Ph.D. Programs in Theatre and English at the Graduate Center of the City University of New York. He has held fellowships from the Fulbright, Rockefeller and Guggenheim foundations and three fellowships from the National Endowment for the Humanities. Among his fourteen books are *An Outline History of American Drama* (1965), *An Emerging Entertainment: The Drama of the American People to 1828* (1977), *Heralds of Promise: The Drama of the American People During the Age of Jackson, 1829-1949* (1986) and a co-edited collection entitled *Modern Drama from Communist China* (1970).

Mollie Ann Meserve is a freelance editor and writer and winner of four national awards for playwriting. For the past eight years, she has compiled *The Playwright's Companion: A Submission Guide to Theatres and Contests in the U.S.A.*

Together, the Meserves are authors of *The Theatre Lover's Cookbook: Recipes from 60 Favorite Plays* (1992).